HIGH TOUCH SELLING

HOW TO MAKE A GREAT LIFE
WHILE MAKING A GREAT LIVING

JOHN SAVAGE, CLU

While a great deal of care has been taken to provide accurate and current information, the ideas, suggestions, general principles, and conclusions presented in this book are subject to local, state, and federal laws and regulations, court cases, and any revisions of same. The reader is thus urged to consult legal counsel regarding any points of law—this publication should not be used as a substitute for competent legal advice.

© 1986 by Longman Group USA Inc.

Published by Farnsworth Publishing Company, a subsidiary of Longman Financial Services Publishing, Inc.

87 88 89   10 9 8 7 6 5 4 3

Library of Congress Cataloging-in-Publication Data

Savage, John.
    High-touch selling.

    1. Insurance, Life—Agents.   2. Selling.
I. Title.
HG8877.S28   1986   368.3'2'00688   86-7487
ISBN 0-88462-678-4

Contents

Dedication

I dedicate this book to Kate, my beautiful wife and mother of nine great children. She exemplifies the ultimate in motherhood with love and understanding for her husband, which is probably much more than I deserve but is greatly appreciated. She is a marvel at time management, engaging in so many duties and performing them so very well. She exemplifies Christianity and sets an example for many young married women to follow. Kate means so very much to me and the children, and I thank God daily for this wonderful miracle in my life. She has great parents, Urban and Margaret Falter, and I thank them deeply for raising a super gal who has fulfilled every dream I have ever had in marriage. May God bless her and keep her for many years to come.

Preface

In his nationally acclaimed book, *Megatrends*, John Naisbitt points out how this nation is moving in the dual direction of high tech/high touch. We are, he notes, matching each new technology with a compensatory human response.

Perhaps wedding "high touch" with "selling" as the title of my book is somewhat presumptuous. In terms of really effective selling, it might even be a redundancy. In *my* book, "effective selling" *is* "high touch" selling. Without the counterbalancing human response to the cold efficiency of the computer (when it's not "down," of course), those very useful illustrations would be deadly in a sales presentation. In my opinion, we must really touch every individual.

In terms of what I'm trying to convey in this book, "high touch" selling means a service-oriented approach to selling, an approach that considers the client's needs of paramount importance. There's nothing startingly new in that, of course. Many of my most successful peers have been doing just that from the start of their careers. But my purpose in writing this book is to tell you how *I* do it.

I hope that you'll benefit from my experiences, observations, and reconstructed interviews. You won't agree with all my views and methods. Nor should you. Pick and choose what suits you, just as I have done through the years in fashioning my own career.

As I have said in many of my talks, I'm not looking for disciples. I just hope that I can serve as a catalyst to help those who seek the answers to both effective selling and effective living.

Acknowledgements

It is important that I take this opportunity to thank all the people who have made the writing of this book possible.

First, I want to thank my wife Kate for allowing me the time to take on this major project.

I thank also:

- my secretaries, Wilma and Lisa, for their excellent work in helping me to free up time to write and lecture.
- my children, because, collectively, they have not given me any problems to distract my attention from this endeavor (which took more than three years).
- my brothers, sisters, and friends for their constant support. I have received further support from my clientele, which has given me financial security as I engage in all of my extracurricular activities.
- Almighty God, for blessing me with a bonus of energy to finish—often when I have bitten off more than I can chew. I'd like to thank especially Dave Drury, my high school and college classmate, who has spent many hours with me in the development of this book, arranging and rearranging my writing.

1

High Touch

Too many people, including those in the insurance industry, fail to appreciate the essential value of making a life while making a living. "High touch" is my capsule term for the process I have evolved throughout most of my career when trying to cope with the challenge of integrating the earning of a comfortable livelihood with the equally important goal of enjoying the fruits of my considerable efforts. It is a slow—sometimes glacially tedious—procedure, which often can be as frustrating as it certainly is rewarding. I know, thanks to 34 years of doing.

"High touch" entails deliberate, thoughtful, ever-considerate contact with the essential people in your life: clients, sales associates, home office personnel, your own office staff, persons with whom you conduct business, family, friends, and you. (Regarding that last contact, if you are not constantly considering yourself—assessing, priming, motivating, improving—you are ignoring an irreplaceable ingredient.)

THE FIVE-STAR CIRCLE

I like to illustrate my "high touch" philosophy with a captioned circle:

1

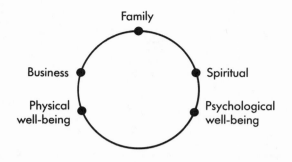

These are the critical bases, in a constantly revolving continuum. Which is the most important? Which is the least? All and none. Operating effectively within each category is an indispensable necessity—not equal all the time, but adequate. (Nobody can effectively sustain a five-way split in concentration.)

I have heard many people state that God is number one, family is second, and their business is third. I am emphatic when I say they all are number one—all five in the preceding circle. Please do not misunderstand me; I am a willing, dedicated person who cherishes his religion. But I also know that unless I awake with the thought of making a living—hitting the floor figuratively running for my professional goals—I am in deep trouble. As I tell my children, if you are boating on Lake Erie and a storm develops, pray to God, but row to shore! Fast! It's not redundant to recognize that the Lord helps those who help themselves.

I want to emphasize the urgency of keeping your "high touch" elements in perspective. If you allow yourself to stress one or more at the expense of the others, you will fracture the circle. This is not to say that one of the five key items will not periodically require special attention. If you have a family problem, a real obstacle, then focus all your attention on that obstacle until it is removed. You must restore your family's equilibrium for its—and your—survival. Whatever interrupts the flow of your circle has to be confronted and eliminated, because the parts to the circle are interdependent. If you lose your grip on one of those parts, the rest will go spinning off out of control. Then you really will be on a chase!

Unfortunately, this delicate balancing act so essential to overall well-being has become infinitely more difficult with the advancement of high tech, of which "high touch" would seem to be the antithesis. Technology has quickly infiltrated virtually every facet of our society, in some instances almost to the point of suffocation. Though I am no reactionary about this ongoing phenomenon—technology is, or at least should be used as, a tool—my concern is that it may use us more than we use it. Many fall into the trap of thinking that high technology, with its admittedly awesome real and potential power, is an insensitive, irresistible force beyond our feeble strengths to understand and utilize. But this is not so, if you work constantly at keeping your own, personal five-starred, "high touch" circle intact. Maintaining this balance certainly is not easy; few things worthwhile are. But I am convinced "high touch" is my best bet in a life John F. Kennedy aptly and simply described as "not fair," and I sincerely hope you will be persuaded it is your best bet as well.

When I started my professional career, it was as a seller of life insurance. I soon discovered that, to survive, I would have to broaden my capabilities and services. So for the past 25 years, I have gradually but deliberately acquired the know-how and techniques to help people obtain the *total* financial planning they have since then come to expect and need. (I'll address this in detail later on.)

For those who have a strong desire to excel, I want to describe the vital steps in a business that is one of confidence-building, a business of dealers in—and buyers of—intangibles that frequently are difficult to explain.

DEVELOPING AS A SALESPERSON

First, to develop as a salesperson, you simply must know what you are doing. Unless you know the details, the finer aspects, the nuances, you cannot hope to communicate as a reliable and believable resource. You cannot hope to close sales and earn a living as an insurance/financial planning agent.

Avoid all exaggerations, even when you are sure you *know* what is good for the buyer. I am certain we all have exaggerated at one time or another—still, I will persist in my belief in the practiced understatement, consciously and purposefully expressed. (This tone should not, however, have an apologetic or hesitant ring—after all, wimps are losers by definition.) I advocate a completely nonarrogant tone reflecting quiet authority; thoughts should be expressed politely but firmly in uncomplicated, direct sentences. I take my cue from the Greatest Teacher, who took all that was complex in the spiritual world and converted it to simple metaphors and parables for the natural world. Even children grasp the meanings of the Bible.

Caution: As you learn to skillfully press home your points and underline the pluses, concede and discuss the weaknesses in whatever you and your client are examining. Everything has flaws, to a lesser or greater degree. Thus you will build confidence for yourself and build a much stronger client relationship if you point out the drawbacks.

Of course, I do not recommend that you dwell excessively on the liabilities in your plan. Just be up-front, honest, truthful. It is your key to being considered *trustworthy*. All we have is trust, and if that trust is violated, we have nothing.

WOULD YOU BUY IT YOURSELF?

Never recommend anything to a client or prospect that you would not consider buying for yourself in comparable circumstances. I have been guided by this principle throughout my career, both within and outside the insurance trade. In this span I formed 23 partnerships, in each of which I was the heaviest investor with, obviously, the greatest risk. To date I have done very well with 18, failed with two, and fared poor-to-weak on three.* Happily for my fellow investors and me, the best brought far greater returns than the bad ones cost in losses. From this experience I developed a stronger appreciation for the philosophy I described above—not trying to sell what you yourself would not buy. I embellished this by anteing up more than

---

*Incidentally, the most successful of the partnerships was a fast-food franchise. So was the worst.

anyone else who gambled with me. I reason that if I persuade others to invest their hard-earned savings, I am personally obliged to put more money at risk than they do. Also, I have gained renewed respect for that old adage against placing too many eggs in a single basket. Following this maxim, the law of averages has more than taken care of me.

Time to get back to the blackboard (and my love affair with circle diagrams):

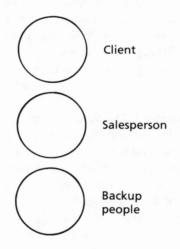

Client

Salesperson

Backup
people

I began by diagramming a five-item circle consisting of "spiritual," "family," and "physical" and "psychological" well-being. The fifth element, "business," is subdivided above into three groupings. The three circles I have drawn above represent, I believe, an approach new to most people in sales. The majority fully understands the importance of "high touch." However, few demonstrate real effectiveness in this relationship. Most neglect to consider "what I think" of equal importance in the "high touch" equation when it comes to their administrative assistants, secretaries, and other backup people. This consideration is vital. First, we all share the human characteristic and would like to be treated with respect. Few things are more offensive (or baffling) to me than the spectacle of a supposed salesperson berating a secretary. I am aghast at seeing how some superiors treat their staffs. Bullies are universally repugnant—that is bad enough.

But what is even worse (the baffling part) is that such insensitive conduct is so counterproductive!—after all, we are, inescapably, members of a team.

INSPIRING TEAMWORK

Teamwork is either success-oriented or doomed for the loss column. Terminology aside, you yourself want and need the gentle "stroking" of "high touch." So does your client. And so do your business associates. Slaves will comply out of fear of the whip. But slavery induced by a sharp tongue breeds resentment and visions of revenge. And if this is not a prescription for a business-gutting backlash, I have never seen one.

Do anything but shout down a colleague. Shout praise. Whisper criticism. And keep the whispering on a positive course. Touch favorably everyone with whom you come in contact. Nobody can do this all the time. But it's the trying that counts. The more you try to be a genuine salesperson—one who undertakes the challenge of first selling himself or herself—the better you will be at it. And so will those whom you contact.

In essence, your job is to serve, not to be served. Keep this foremost in mind as I offer you the perspectives I have accumulated on selling effectiveness.

2

Goal Setting

When setting your goals, think big—not extravagant or unlimited—big as opposed to small, overly cautious, hesitant. Little plans lack the magic that stirs the blood and have about as much chance for success as their size. There is risk associated with big goals. But there is some risk in *any* goal—and if you are not willing to take risks, you should not be in the game. I have seen too many who have *never* had the thrill of testing themselves with a long stretch on a limb. Their careers are oriented around the self-induced fear of failure. How dull. And how sad, to have fear dictate and compromise the healthy, normal desire to succeed.

So reach out toward the stars. If you fall short, reach again. Adjust your sights to reality—but don't grab the security blanket and suck your thumb. That's for tots who are in a protected environment but do not realize it. Your environment is *not* protected. You are in a jungle. (And tigers have a way of eating up thumb-sucking blanket-huggers.) Besides, goal-setting is one of the best ways I know to "stroke" yourself psychologically.

I have developed a goal-setting formula over the years that has held me in good stead. It consists of five parts, all separate from the determination to feel good about myself most of the time. Let me dissect the collective goals one by one.

500 LIVES A YEAR

First, I consider it important to have precise objectives for surpassing those of the previous year in premiums, volume, new clients, and overall dollar income. And my number one target is the new lives I sell, with this year's goal at 400. To these I aim to add 100 new clients to my client file. These I intend to translate into new premium dollars, written as follows: $500,000 on ordinary life sales, $1,000,000 on annuity sales, and $30,000 on disability income premiums. In sum, this year's Savage reach will be for $100,000,000 in new business, personally, with an overall *insurance* income of $500,000, of which one-fifth will be derived from renewals. My business cost of operation? Roughly $60,000 for the year.

I must emphasize that my goals do *not* include "accumulation." I am not interested in acquiring money for the sake of it. I am *very* interested in challenging myself to leap beyond my most recent past performance—every year I am alive. That leap I call "reaching," which I find essential to good practice.

But how does a person decide what is too long or short a "reach"? Your stretch should be attainable. You will be more satisfied in the long run with a goal that is achievable, if modest, than with a goal that looks great on paper but is unrealistic.

Savage's rough translation: If you are at 50 lives, don't shoot for 300 lives—shoot for 100. If your past year was 100, set your sights to 150. From 150, your target should be 200. *Then*, once you have reached the 200 plateau, your new goal should be 300. What if you hit the 300 mark? Then try 350, right? Wrong. Try *500* new lives. You can do it and will!

SELLING IN YOUR OFFICE

I carry through on my self-pledges by conducting all meetings with clients at my office. Over the past 20 years, 90 percent of my client discussions have been held where I work. Over the past five years, my office interviews have constituted 99 percent of the total. For time-treasuring efficiency, this routine cannot be equaled.

And make no mistake, efficiency is increasingly important. It is totally unacceptable to write 30 to 50 lives per year—you must write a minimum of 100 and should actually be closer to 200. So you must conduct a high number of interviews. The odds have to be in your favor, and the more you exercise your techniques, the sharper you will be.

When thinking about prospecting, ignore the destructive myth about working a special market; for example, concentrating on business people, blue-collar workers, professional types, etc. Every *worker* is a prospect. In my opinion, there is only one valid test in this regard: whether the potential contact is or is not gainfully employed.

Many agents eventually can do very well by working with a full mix of clients of the same age. Some clients inevitably will wind up at the top of the financial ladder. And guess who will be well known to them. That's right—you will!

Again, though, avoid the blinders. Times change so often that you would need more wisdom than Solomon to accurately envision the future. Consider a few examples of how our world—and the occupations in it—has changed. The store that only ten years ago sold manual typewriters is a computer center today. Yesterday's family doctor can frequently be found in a professional association today, practicing with his or her peers in a number of specialties. The downtown stores have been replaced by shopping malls. Thousands of corporate executives have been given "golden handshakes" and are either retired or self-employed consultants. Times do change—and prospecting in a specific area can ultimately be disastrous. If you spread yourself around all manner of prospects, you not only will greatly enhance your insurance business, you also will construct the underpinnings of a successful adventure in total financial planning.

NEW CLIENTS ARE IMPORTANT

My goal of having 100 new clients who are not in my client file is a practical recognition of the peril in leaning on old clients—too often the pattern in our business. Time and again we sell the business owners and totally neglect the employees. Ironically, you can be lulled into thinking high volume with existing clientele is more than adequate—while you permit the erosion of potential new sales. Always broaden your base with new clients each year. It is easy if you work at it. You will get referrals from the most important source: your own *satisfied, trusting* clientele.

COLD CALLS

A Note on Cold Calling

In the preface, I warned you that you will not agree with everything I say (nor should you!). Let me insert a very personal feeling about "cold calls." I have never made a cold call in my professional life—and it has been decades since I tried direct mail. My first (and only) attempt at direct mail was, to put it lightly, an unmitigated disaster. It came at a time when I was struggling to overcome the onus of being what I call "a successful failure." It was at a time when I had been in the business for nine years and was making only $5,000 per year. But if cold calls work for you, go on making them. If direct mail brings in sufficient business, use it. I know many agents are very successful with those two methods—but I am not one of them.

A Note on Premiums

"Premium"—there was a time the word was not worth mentioning. Now the premium income dollar is so low it necessitates a high goal to warrant the chase. Nevertheless, it is in your best interests to pursue this rabbit for the balance it can provide your income mix. For example, my $1.2 million in annuities last year earned me $27,500—a nice, tidy plus. But this rabbit is fleet of foot, with all sorts of off-spring. Shoot for the biggest and most in the bunch.

A Note on Volume

Volume has been my motivator for 20 years. (It is woven among many of the sentences you have already read here.) Volume is a worthwhile concern. It pays—and it is a productive way to collect company accolades, which can be rewarding.

Make your business world one of insurance *and* finance. Each year strive to do better than the year before. Assume that you will be rewarded for your efforts and you probably will not be disappointed. I believe that in finance, honest effort is almost invariably rewarded financially. Moreover, simply living by that credo—naive as it may sound—heightens our chances of success.

Granted, our vocation imposes periods of denial and nose-grinding. But in a land of free enterprise, opportunity knocks continually for those willing to respond.

Of course, the assumption is that you have been trained properly so that you will be able to capitalize on opportunities. Unfortunately, that is not the case with many of our contemporaries. This leads to the question of whether you are a hunter or a trapper.

HUNTERS AND TRAPPERS

Most of us who have been selling for a while were trained as (insurance) hunters. By this I mean that we were indoctrinated in the practice of stalking our "prey." Plodding through a field, we covered countless miles in the hope of a steady, clean shot at a specific target. We checked the wind, rustled the bushes, held our breath, wore ourselves out, and congratulated ourselves if we could bring home anything to show for our exhaustion.

But our industry has changed, as has the whole world of finance. Unfortunately for literal hordes in our business, however, the news has not caught up to them. Or if it has, they seem to be unable or unwilling to adjust. Now is the day of the (insurance) trapper, but admitting as much makes it necessary to change bad habits that are rooted in past training.

Because we all are creatures of (often slaves to) habit, as were our professional predecessors, breaking the pattern will be tough. Even the most astute are wedded to highly conditioned reflexes, down to the ritual of how to shave, shower, put on shoes, enter a car, and on and on. And experts estimate normal habit change requires at least 30 days. In any case, while the (insurance) hunter approach of the past half-century may have sufficed, that methodology is *dead*—and the corpse has yet to receive a fit burial.

Before I describe (insurance) trapping, I am going to try hammering some long spikes in that hunter's coffin. A short while ago I was speaking in Portland, Oregon, on this very subject. At break time, a young fellow asked me, almost pleadingly, if I would amplify my point about people being creatures of habit. I first complimented him for taking the time to inquire, reviewed some of my main points on the virtue of broadening one's search for customers—and then asked him to describe his work regimen.

The answer was as unnerving as it probably is all too typical. The young man said he showed up at the office at roughly 10 in the morning, talked things over with his colleagues, then went to lunch for up to an hour-and-a-half. After lunch he set to work. He was candid enough to admit his half-days were not very productive. Aside from the 10 a.m. start, the breeze-shooting with fellow agents, and the leisurely lunch, he was the equivalent of an "ambulance-chaser": cold calls to newlyweds, hot calls to relatives. He would follow up an engagement announcement or the opening of a new business. He essentially sniffed, hunted, and fired at anything that moved in the field—at the same time that armies of hunters were firing at the same rifled bodies, fighting for the million-to-one chance. I have never prospected among nonreferrals, neighbors, fellow church-goers, or anyone else where my unexpected approach would even suggest the possibility of an embarrassment (either for them or me). One of the worst tags a salesperson can be labeled with is that of a pushy pest. It is to a salesperson what pollution is to a stream. Besides gumming up his or her own presentation and breaking relationships that can never be mended, the vulture among us soils the sales reputation in general. These people are all gears and no levers, guided and possibly inspired by a training manual conjuring dreams of instant success and gratification. But once they try to sell to people other than cousins, aunts, uncles, etc. (with whom they may be "relatively" successful), they are soon added to the sales mortality rate—with yet another of their kind elbowing in to join in the hunt.

THE NEW BREED: TRAPPERS

Enter the trapper, the opposite of the hard-charging, aggressive, energy-wasting, annihilation-prone (and suicidal) hunter. Who/what is this new breed of insurance/finance professional? The dominant industry force for at least the next 20 years, that's who. And the breed is not all that new, either. But make no mistake, the trappers will be the survivors as well as the leaders.

Before examining trappers more closely, however, I would like to digress momentarily to examine that charismatic quality, "leadership."

As I observe our society, I find that people fall into three categories. Five percent get up every morning intending to lead by good example, continue a quality lifestyle, be dutiful, and maintain integrity. Another five percent get up bent on doing just the opposite. I have no problem with either, so long as I know who they are. My problem comes with the 90 percent who start off the day shrugging their shoulders, willing to be led by either group.

The newspapers are full of stories. Leaders take many forms. We are attracted to some; we are repelled by others. For good cause or evil, victory goes to the leaders who are determined, persevering, imaginative, and innovative, and who can accurately assess needs and fulfill them.

We can either lead or be led, and choosing to lead encompasses a fairly awesome array of demands even for those who manage to succeed as leaders. In my profession I have for a long time chosen to lead. You can, too, if you have the instincts and drive to be a trapper.

Unlike the narrow-gauge hunters, the trappers cover the field like a blanket. Everything that moves and has an income is fair game. Trappers are not interested in a specific species during a given season. Their traps are laid out methodically in every direction. They do not chase and wear themselves out in the process.

Trappers allow their methods to work for them, returning routinely and regularly to determine what their traps have produced. They are everywhere at once, while hunters are in one place at a time, with access only to what is in that part of the field at that given moment. Trappers bag everything from little to enormous, appreciating the fact that their smaller catches will develop and prosper, some growing into huge assets. Hunters may not necessarily disdain the smaller catches, but they do not share trappers' determination to court the small fry; they do not have real interest or patience—or sense of truly productive strategy. The life of the trapper is infinitely more rewarding and, conversely, less exerting.

ALMOST PERFECT RESULTS

Here is how I compare the results achieved by the hunter and the trapper, based on my experience:

	Number of Calls	Number of Interviews	Number of Sales
Hunter	10	3	1
Trapper	10	10	10

Is ten out of ten realistic? I believe it to be. Last year only four of my appointments did not result in a sale. *My goal for this year (and every year) is not to have a single "no-sale."* Through the first quarter of this year, I had one failure. My goal is to have that be my *only* failure. Next year I will shoot for the perfect clean slate. I may not make it. Maybe it cannot be done, especially in a high volume call-and-interview atmosphere. But as a "high-touch" trapper, someone will have to carry me out feet first before I will stop trying for a spotless year.

Compare my goal and actual performance with the typical hunters, with their one-out-of-ten record. One-for-ten is pitifully poor in practically any endeavor—and it is also a pitifully poor way to make a living.

Hunters must constantly recharge themselves psychologically for the quick kill; but successful trappers are those who always take time to understand themselves and to honestly try to know how others perceive them. There are subtle but major differences in how you self-evaluate what others say about you—and what they really think of you.

I had a staggering introduction to this evaluation process at the age of 25. I had been shooting baskets one day at Toledo's near-downtown Catholic club. Out of the clear I was beckoned to a corner of the gym by the club's director, Monsignor Jerome Schmitt, as wonderful a person as I have ever met.

Imagine my face, spine, and knees as the Monsignor hit me with this: "You are the most selfish guy I have ever seen." I had been thinking I was pretty great stuff, living the good life, liked by one and all, a responsible guy. Then, in one blunt, totally unexpected salvo, a living saint pegged me as the "most selfish" thing in shoe leather. But bless him forever for at least thinking enough of my self-centered hide to brace me as I had never been stiffed before, or since. He put the mirror to my mug and made me see, for the first time, what others saw but hadn't the guts or interest to tell me. Maybe they wanted to but didn't know how. The good Monsignor came, saw, and conquered.

SERVING OTHERS

Thereafter I guess I did as close to a 180-degree turnaround as is humanly possible. I became very active in the Catholic Youth Organization and, over the years, scores of other service-oriented organizations and activities. Not for them. For *me*. Because I learned rapidly that in serving others, especially those with special needs, I best serve myself, my self-concept. I feel wonderful about it. The more I truly give of myself, the better I feel. So, know yourself.

If you haven't given yourself the incredible benefit of helping—serving—others, I urge you to throw yourself into one or more worthy causes that fit your unique abilities. You will never regret it. Quite likely, you desperately need to do it to break your self-delusion, as mine was shattered by a gutsy priest when I was in my mid-20s. I was lucky to have been set straight at that early age. Maybe you weren't or aren't so fortunate. Sit yourself down for a good talking to. Analyze your life with brutal candor. Then you will start understanding what others not only say but think about you as a person whose existence depends on trust, confidence, respect, and integrity. It worked for me. Five years after that priestly encounter, my sales began to take off. Genuine, consistent "high touch" with everyone with whom I came in contact, plus my trapper's mentality, have given me the career equivalent of walks in space. Try it.

Be just as honest and thorough in critiquing your office environment. Is it dedicated to "hunting" principles that time and common sense have deserted? Is the pattern irreversible, allowing no leeway or patience for you as a trapper? If so, my firm advice to you is to leave it and find the compatible environment you require to succeed. If you stay you will rapidly wear out trying to compete against elite organizations that, I guarantee, will reap 90 percent of the sales with ten percent of the talent. You have to decide whether you want to make a life or a living. Most people make a living. But how many are making a great life?

When switching from hunting to trapping in selling, or coming in as a beginner, however, you have to understand fully that combing a total society places an enormous premium on patience. Such an operation takes time to hit its maximum efficiency. Work your base— present yourself professionally and referrals will follow. In time, those traps will be snapping closed.

3

Management

I was in a management position for more than 15 years and assisted in management for three years prior to that. I am also aware of the many clichés directed toward business leadership. A wag once said that to err is human, to err constantly is management. Although this is more humorous than accurate, it does contain an element of truth. One of the functions of management is to make decisions—and no one can bat 1,000 at decision-making. We tend to dwell on the decisions that went awry while forgetting those that were right on the money. But in my opinion, the quality of management poses one of the major challenges in our industry today.

A lot of good training takes place in our business. However, a good deal of "training" takes place that is unproductive, myopic, and of poor quality. Some of it amounts to force-feeding.

In the past decade I have spoken more than 300 times at 56 home-office conventions, at seminars for everybody from athletes and coaches, to administrators and educators from London to Japan. Among various impressions left with me is that of the deplorable state of management training. I define education as a learning process, something acquired through reading, going to school, observing, and experiencing. Training is what you experience face-to-face, day-by-day at your workplace. In contradiction is the manager who feels management's responsibility for training consists of packing an agent or employee off, somewhere, for a week's seminar.

WINNING—AND LOSING—MANAGEMENT

People manage *things*. But they *lead* people. The most critical ingredient in the leadership formula is investing the time required to select promising salespersons. Look at successful coaches. They spend as much time recruiting as they do coaching, scouring the landscape for their unique blend of talent, character, perseverance, teamwork, and strength.

But in our business, even when recruiting produces the right combination in a novice, the natural intensity offered by the solid new prospect is all too frequently allowed to dissipate. His or her superior fails to follow through with adequate training and timely stroking. Here is an athlete-coaching analogy. The winning coach starts preparing the squad months before the season starts. The coach knows exactly how much has to be covered to reach the comfort zone between practice and game. The coach leads the team. Always!

Coaches never relinquish their roles, overlook flaws or tolerate apathy or indecision. Their intensity is always at fever pitch. It has to be if they hope to make that fever contagious. We all can learn from watching how a good coach operates.

I am just finishing my 35th year as an insurance salesman in Toledo, Ohio. I was a little unnerved when a colleague brought to my attention the fact that he and I constituted a skimpy minority of fewer than ten agents in our area who started together and who have survived in the profession to date. When you look around for comparable figures on doctors, lawyers, educators—name the profession—the career mortality rate in our business is nothing short of abominable. We are talking apples and oranges, yes, but we should be retaining more of the people we recruit. A management compensation system that accentuates long-term development of salespeople—instead of just recruiting—can do wonders in providing a solution to this problem.

Salespeople look to managers for leadership, for emphasis more on practice than on preaching, and for role-model relationships. When we look at successful management leaders, we see a number of qualities: We see people who are healthy, who practice moderation in diet, who exercise frequently, who dress well but not ostentatiously, who are interested in their appearance not for reasons of vanity but for professional purposes, and who are genuinely interested in the success of the people they have brought into life insurance.

I have been a trainer/educator/coach inside and outside formal education settings, in schools, and in the office. The experience has given me tremendous satisfaction. There is nothing like knowing you had a hand in the development of young people, seeing many trainees become life members of the Million Dollar Club. I can imagine the sentiments of a great teacher of pianists as opposed to the feelings of a great performer. The former can see the fruits of his labor in scores of concert halls.

Of course, not everyone is cut out to be a great trainer. But in our business the potential for achieving exemplary trainers is lessened even further by policies that ignore the urgency of properly training the trainers.

The life insurance business, by virtue of the needed protection and financial products it offers, is today alive and, by appearances, well. And as I see it, the future is very bright for well-trained, experienced practitioners. They have always understood that selling conceptually is what counts. I sometimes wonder, though, if "the message" has gotten through to others such as some field managers and some home office officials. A number of these people appear to be overly concerned about product, overlooking the fact that products in our business do not sell themselves. Salespeople sell them. And to be effective, salespeople need training so that they can communicate the benefits of the products to their clients and demonstrate their need for these great products. The chain of client-agent-management-product developer is what has to be analyzed and strengthened. The "weakest link" analogy has never been more true than in this chain. The public leads us to discover what its needs are. Being closest to the public, the agent carries the message back to those responsible for product development. The developers have to produce a product that is attractive, saleable, and competitive. Management has to train the agents in the features of the product and how to sell it and it is the agent's responsibility to sell the product. When any link of this chain fails, nothing gets sold, the public does not get served, and the agent does not earn one dollar. This whole point may seem obvious to many readers but I think it sometimes gets lost as it travels "up the chain."

Our trainees have to start obtaining the training they must have if the industry is to prosper. As soon as they have been recruited they should be advised they are in a profession that relies on long-lasting relationships, that their profession is a tough business, that self-denial is an essential part of it, that they need to be all ears (which pre-supposes their training is sufficiently thorough and interesting enough to hold their attention). Trainees must be treated honestly. It is shameful for a manager to imply that a beginner automatically will become a million-dollar producer. Such an implication should be qualified by a factor of, say, one in ten.

Discipline and self-denial are essential within and outside the office. I am neither stoic nor Spartan, but I genuinely respect the principle that great things come from harnessing our indulgences. It is not surefire (what is?) but there are gold nuggets of truth in the old maxim, "Early to bed and early to rise makes a man healthy, wealthy, and wise."

WHAT IS GOOD TRAINING?

A while ago I was invited to visit an insurance home office and review one of its training procedures. In one instance the trainees were supposedly being indoctrinated in the art of telephone proce-dure. They were taken along, step by step, in a ritual consisting of tips they were to incorporate by talking at a dead instrument. I was a little upset. What an exercise! A beginner learns to talk with pros-pects via telephone by *talking* with prospects via telephone. And if the smarts exist, they will emerge in gradually improved perfor-mance, on the phone and across the desk.

The visit reminded me of my first stint as an instructor in public speaking. I looked at the text I was supposed to use. Its introduction contained an extensive, medically framed description of vocal chords and larynx. I threw it away and got on with the process of teaching my students how to speak in public. By the end of the semester, even the nervous students felt comfortable speaking in front of the class. They learned and achieved because I attacked not their ignorance but their fear. You cannot do this by outlining telephone etiquette/tech-

niques. You learn by replacing fear with confidence and composure—
by doing. This is the trick to be taught by the truly knowledgeable
trainer.

I also taught—rather than coached—basketball. And I focused
on what every trainee deserves: a close look at the basics—why they
are basic and why they are important. It was essential that I focus
energy on these basics, for without a solid base, everything layered
atop it is in jeopardy. I would ask, "Why doesn't a player have to
look at a basketball while he is dribbling?" I would hear such answers
as, "You can see the defense," or "You have full-court vision," after
which I would halt the answering: "The reason you don't have to
look at a basketball while dribbling is because it is *round*. If you
drop it, it will come straight back up. If I asked you to dribble a
football, now *that* would be different. You'd really have to keep your
eyes on the ball."

Many times, in both my writing and lectures, I use the word
"balance." It is probably more important in the trainer's charge than
anything else. For 35 years I have been telling people they do not
have to work 20 hours a day. Work eight hours, sleep eight—just
make sure they aren't the same eight!

I believe that too many trainers load their trainees with too much
to comprehend in too short a time. Training a new agent is a long,
tedious job. Anyone who is unwilling to give it the time and dedication should get out of management.

Undoubtedly, at first blush insurance companies figure their
management team is doing a great job. The same goes for the public's
impression of its own practitioners. But nothing lasts forever. And
the signal I am trying to send is that our industry had better reexamine
its training levels and begin to streamline them. For years, the geo-
metric growth of our country kept pushing up our production results.
That day is over. It's gone!

It is too late when, after rolling along smoothly under the
appreciative eye of the company, production suddenly takes a pre-
cipitous dive. It is too late when, in a frantic search for answers and
solutions, the company representatives come to the only place that
counts—the field—and find a shambles.

What then? Can companies fall back on the professional sports
gambit of shelling out tons of money to buy an established star? Or

buy some experienced agents? This is no solution—just a loose Band
Aid at a major surgery price. Smart baseball managers know that
their futures lie in their farm systems and in the minor leagues. They
know their top talent will eventually fizzle out and that their salvation
rests with the youngsters down the ladder and with the coaches whose
job it is to extract every ounce of skill in them.

OUR REAL CONCERN

I suggest that in the next five years the real concern in our
business will be coping with the accelerated demand to provide total
financial planning. To this predictable end we must recruit and train
a sharp army of highly educated, highly motivated individuals.

If you are inclined to agree with me that our trainee training
can be grossly deficient, think also about our *continuing* education.
It is almost nonexistent. And that problem exists not only here on
our side of the pond—it is everywhere. I say this from the hindsight
of looking at my hometown, going all across our nation, and seeing
what's going on overseas. I also offer this as a credential:

In 1960, the agency of which I was a part had a $4,000,000
volume on less than $50,000 of premium. When I took over the
Columbus Mutual office in Toledo we had 50 agents licensed to sell,
most of whom were part-timers (policeman, milkman, you name it).
Four of us were making what could charitably be called a living.
After carefully examining my forces, I knew changes were essential.
If I were to have a professional agency, it would have to start acting
like one. I made sure I talked with every agent, every day, and found
that, for the first time in their lives, they were getting much-needed
recognition.

In 25 years that shambles evolved. Toledo is a city that has had
more than its share of unemployment and expansion misses, yet our
office now has 41 agents and will produce more than one-half billion
dollars in new life insurance sales, with premiums of $3,000,000.

I am not saying we are number one in the United States in
premium or volume. What I am saying is that upon close examina-
tion, when it comes to quality of personnel, education, training, and

office environment, I believe we are one of the best in the country. During the past year more than 30 agents visited to observe our operation. I am as proud of that as I am willing to share our experience and procedure. It also allows me to spend a great deal of time on the road, preaching sound training and client development to anyone who has the intelligence to appreciate what is happening (or not happening) in the industry to which he or she has made a commitment.

MY TWO VISITORS

The above brings me to the recollection of two young visitors from the West I allowed to come and observe how I work. As is my pattern in such a circumstance, I paid for their stay at a nearby hotel, with the clear stipulation that I am not a tour guide—no trips to the art museum, or the waterfront, or the glass factories, or the coal port. I work; they observe. That is all.

Both were in their early 30s and had been doing a creditable job but felt they had not progressed as far as they could or should. They had heard me speak at a Million Dollar Round Table meeting and decided they wanted to follow up with visits to two other speakers and me. As it turned out, I was last on their schedule.

On their third day with me, I invited them for a home-cooked meal. As we sat around the table chatting, one turned to my wife and said, "Mrs. Savage, when we compare your husband's operation with the others we visited for three days each, we found he's the only one who is working the way he talks about working." What a sad commentary. These young men, wanting to upgrade, willing to pay the price, traveled to learn and listened to three men speak. What they said sounded good. But when these young men went to see they found personalities different from what they had heard. I guess that is why I continue to give speeches around the country, to help get the word to young agents who are anxiously trying, in many instances, to survive.

What about the future? I believe it has never been clearer and the potential has never been greater. By my nature, I am a positive person (some feel too positive). I do not think it is possible to be too positive. Business will continue to go where invited and remain where appreciated.

And what about prospects? Prospects are waiting to be approached by a well-trained, decent-looking agent who can effectively communicate his or her knowledge and concern to the degree they are convinced he or she really cares. Cares, that is, to build a relationship that will last, to be there to address the many changes that lie ahead in the world of financial planning.

To prepare a young person to fit this role does not just happen. Sales trainers will have to work three times as hard as they have in the past. They will have to demand and acquire a thorough knowledge of all financial instruments. This, of course, begins with a complete upgrading of the trainers' own knowledge through conscientious study.

The trainer also will have to remain in daily touch with the trainees. He or she cannot depend on the home office, which is not and should not be equipped to train. What the home office should provide are thoughtful, productive guidelines, tools, systems, and services.

WHERE THE CHANGE WILL COME

If you think home offices will change instantaneously and become equipped with all the professional backups that have been so painfully absent, you are wrong. This takes time, money, and talent, all of which are frequently in short supply.

The big change, which must come quickly, has to occur in the field with on-the-job training—motivating and educating every new agent to ensure that agent knows what to do before going out in the field. This begins the process. It is followed by surveillance, patience, and understanding from trainers who not only are prepared but *able* to help.

Because some home offices have eliminated all recruiting and training of new field people, there is only one way: concentrating on developing a quality, professional operation at the field level, stressing great selection, great education, and great training. These are the musts for introducing new agents to a successful career. Experience has taught me this for three-and-a-half decades. It is quite clear to me what is needed.

I am also concerned with the tendency, in the past several years, for some companies to intensify their dedication to the bottom line. Their future is this year's upcoming annual report. Research can wait. They find it easiest to fire employees when they want to show a higher profit margin to keep stockholders happy. But for how long? *That is* the question not enough folks are asking.

Look at the typical corporate organization chart and the chain of command it represents. There is a rectangle at the top for the chief executive, a vertical line extending downward—then to right and left—connecting to other boxes, that is, to other high-echelon officers. Under these are more boxes representing a descending order of administrators and their various responsibilities. Work is delegated from top to bottom. Everything and everybody fits in its and their places. Neatly, orderly, and I believe, *counterproductively*.

Why so? Because it is impossible to manage a business if the top executive's *philosophy* is separated by organizational makeup from each employee in the company. The only way the "boss's" philosophy—the rationale for the company's existence—can be transmitted is for that person to communicate individually with every worker in his force. It does not matter whether the number is 12 or 12,000. Moreover, it is a responsibility that cannot be delegated. If there is no philosophy to pass along, if there is no fundamental way to operate down to the lowest level in the organization, then that company must find itself a new chief executive quickly. The dispersion of top-level philosophy is inseparable from the achievement of greater productivity.

You may have read *In Search of Excellence*, which zeroed in on and analyzed six very successful businesses. From my stand-point there is a seventh business operation that deserves study.

This business is an Ohio family-run operation that is without question the best I have ever seen. It is The Andersons, one of the largest partnerships in the U.S. and one of the largest grain shippers anywhere. Its philosophy was established a generation ago by its founder, the much-respected Harold Anderson, and perpetuated by his five sons and a daughter, and has since then been carried like an

Olympic torch by their children. The Andersons has approximately 1,000 employees on its payroll.

Their philosophy is embedded in honesty, a characteristic the partnership extolls as the entire organization's prime duty. Their philosophy also incorporates a sense of caring about people I have yet to see matched. This pattern of behavior is constantly promulgated— so much so that, for a while, I thought The Andersons talked more about philosophy than about productivity.

But I had been missing the real beauty of what managing partner Dick Anderson was accomplishing. He and his top colleagues, through patience and unshakable dedication to their very high principles, had assembled the finest group of employees obtainable and indoctrinated them with the partnership's deep sense of caring for people.

I am left with the belief that, if a thousand-staff, beehive operation like The Andersons can be run so caringly and productively, it can be emulated at any size. And it can be duplicated so much easier where the work force ranges between 50 and 100. It can, should, and will be done if corporate USA is to compete.

4

Building a Clientele

I find incredible the widespread failure to recognize that the key to successful selling is the building of a clientele. I say this in the wake of attending 40 training seminars conducted by as many different companies. Not once did I hear any reference to this all-important process. Over the past few years, with the advent of the universal life product, large numbers of insurance sales people went after millions of dollars of existing life insurance, eroding its cash values, with the cry: "Let me double your insurance coverage at no additional cost." Wait, I cautioned myself—it is time for reality, as well as repetitive reinforcement of the basic building blocks of our client relationships.

Let us review a number of these items:

Item. Every policyholder should be—no, must be—a client in the full and true sense of the word.

Item. Never categorize clients by income or amount of insurance purchased. If they are good enough to earn a living, that is the only criterion required for the provision of your best service. Keep in mind that when you put a price tag on something, its value generally goes down.

This adage applies to the tendency to undervalue clients who are just beginning to work. In my second year in this business, I sold a $5,000 policy to a young friend. Today this same individual has ten million dollars in force with me. Had I stalked bigger game or failed to maintain contact and serve this client's needs, that ten million dollars worth of coverage would have gone to another agent.

DEALING WITH COMPETITION

Item. Do not try to sell with the idea that your product is "the least expensive." Every day somebody offers a "better" buy and/or a realigned set of services. You cannot hope to zig as often as the competition zags. This has nothing to do with doing the right job for your client. You must recognize competitive thrusts, acknowledge them (by keeping up with your industry), and then counter quietly, but firmly, with your product and what is behind it—*you.*

Item. Avoid the "butterfly syndrome," flitting about to land on a different company in order to secure a deceptively appealing first-year commission. It is a deception that undercuts clients and taints the meaning of the word "professional." Ultimately, it is the essence of self-defeat. The butterfly has a demonstrably short flight pattern— and life span.

Item. You may ask how fast one can build a clientele. Rather slowly. The race of life is won not by the swift but by the sure. I did not begin to shift from being "an insurance seller" to being "a client builder" until I had been in the business nine years. The dawn came when I had paid five dollars to attend a business seminar in Cleveland and was exposed to my first primer on client/agent relationships. It was the best money I ever spent. It prompted a self-evaluation that concluded that, while I sold many people, I kept in touch with few.

CHANGES IN MY LIFE

I came home with a set of mixed determinations. I would (1) get married, (2) stop working weekends as a butcher in my dad's grocery store, (3) drop my coaching and teaching jobs, (4) sell the casualty end of my business—all $30,000 worth of it, and (5) sell a little sporting-goods operation I had formed with a pal, Jack Kennedy, and split the $900 we had realized from the (ad)venture. Then, or so the multiple promises went, I would faithfully follow the vision I had seen in Cleveland.

My initial vow, in pursuing my quest for client building, was to see each of my then 150 clients every two to three years. That was in 1959. Within six years, I had turned the corner and was producing well. By 1968 it became painfully apparent that many, many people needed much, much help in managing their financial affairs. That realization led to my dive into the invigorating pool of total financial planning. The year 1968 also was the year in which I concentrated on conducting appointments in my office. My one-on-one client contact rate for a year (800 clients) then started to grow and is now at 90 percent.

WHERE MOST SALES COME FROM

My annual client reviews take place in the five months of January, February, May, September, and October. Coincidentally, these same months produce 75 percent of my insurance income—derived from old, loyal clients. Five months often produce three-fourths of the income obtainable from this source.

Item. Here is another important point: I cannot avoid reiterating about how *not* to build a clientele. It would be improper for me to suggest that you eliminate from your client-building methodologies door-to-door calls, be it for business or individual prospecting. However, I suggest that you examine referral selling; you may find it much more pleasing and certainly easier on your nervous system. There is nothing wrong with picking up the telephone to call a person who has started a business or was just married. Many people have made a very good living using this method. I personally do not use this tactic, although I would agree it offers some potential. For calling just to be calling, however, I don't agree. As for direct mailing, it totally escapes me how anyone who sends 1,000 letters and receives 14 replies can be happy with the results or think that he or she is making good progress. Of course, don't change what you are doing, if you are doing well. Just give thought to adding some of these ideas to your already effective methods. Keep your eye on the doughnut and not on the *hole*. In any case, I firmly believe you cannot beat building by referrals from satisfied clients.

One definition of a friend is someone who knows you well and likes you anyway. I started with about 20 friends who were interested in my welfare and who had the ability and desire to "sell" me to their friends and acquaintances—to folks I did not know at all. I can look back and count an even dozen who were significantly helpful in this regard. And that was all I needed to pyramid to my present substantial clientele.

STARTING YOUNG TO SELL INSURANCE

The question is always raised about the correlation between the age of an agent and the potential for effective client building. My candid observation is that the optimum years for starting an insurance career are 21 to 25. My office has brought in 20 trainees within this age group who earned $40,000 a year. In a word, they were *successful*. Yes, there are many very successful General Agents who have brought in agents over 30, married, with family; and for years LIMRA has advocated this methodology. I would be the last to be critical of LIMRA, but my 30 years in management have demonstrated to me that it is much easier if an agent begins at age 21— for by the time the agent is 30, he or she has already established a clientele and has had the opportunity to mature. I must say I also am partial to the unmarried trainee. Demands on the young married couple are substantially greater than on the single person. The solo trainee has far less *need* for income, regardless of wants. Generally, he or she is more capable of accepting those initial, tough years with their heavy demands on denial and discipline.

For me, the "school of hard-knocks" experience spawned a number of valuable lessons. Spinning my wheels forced me to look into where I stood with my clients. Tortuous, wasted time revealed the futility of undergirding cold calls. But nothing has matched the revelation I experienced 17 years ago when I was hospitalized and bedridden for six months. This adversity was the catalyst for the most dramatic change in my business. My client-friends came to me, to my bedside! They—and my faith—kept me going. When I got back on my feet, they came to my office. The routine set in. To my delight, I discovered that my clients actually preferred this arrangement, no matter what their occupations or professions. The corporate executive liked the change of scenery. For the blue-collar worker and wife, an evening appointment was a night out, to be capped by a restaurant dinner. For me, on top of the touching friendship that inspired it, my office appointment policy sky-rocketed my productivity as well as my ability to serve my burgeoning clientele more closely and routinely.

5

Total Financial Planning

Chapter 5 is the longest chapter in this book. I believe you will find it to be the most valuable and instructional in helping you expand your income by way of teaching your clients the marvels of mature, no-nonsense, educated thrift.

In doing so I am predicting as best I can the trends of the next 15 years. Although I do not want to come across as a Cassandra to those in the business of stocks and bonds, mutual funds, real estate investments, and so on, my outlook nevertheless *is* predicated on a ten-year odyssey that includes visits to every state in the Union, lectures at 30 universities, and stops in 20 countries. In the past two years I have huddled with the heads of state of three nations, parleyed with Singapore's finance minister, attended many seminars, conversed with countless corporate executives, investment counselors, and the like, and have come to this unabashed, unleavened, unhappy conclusion: When it comes to money, *nobody* has a decent grasp of the future. Your guess is, for all practical purposes, as good as all the treasurers, economists, financiers, and fortune tellers put together. It's like trying to foretell the weather along the Great Lakes for Spring, 1995. Any Ohioan in that area is tickled to get a reliable weather reading three *days* hence.

Faced with this condition, the only operative word for sensible financial planning is "conservative." Play your projections close to the vest. My interpretation: For the next 15 years, at least, concentrate on savings *versus* investments.

Let me illustrate the moral and the hazard of investing in the unforeseeable future as opposed to encouraging your clients to safeguard their money in plain old savings deposits. Those who counseled investments in oil, coal, and gas ten years ago can now assess the damage of many of those worthy gambles that ended up as losers. What has become of those fearless forecasters? (What has become of their trusting clients?) Never advise your client to apply his or her money where you would not or will not invest yours.

My emphasis, here and hereafter, will be on savings in the traditional sense of the term. If you absorb what I am going to say, I believe you will have the formula for significant self-progression based on the financial successes achieved by those you counsel. By the time we have finished with this exercise, we will have traveled through some pretty complex territory to arrive at what I think are some surprisingly simple conclusions. (But you are going to have to bear with an array of my friends, the circles.)

LEARNING VS. THINKING

Although I have great respect for education and for educators, I think some of us were shortchanged on the matter of being taught to learn as opposed to being taught to think. Learning the mechanics of how to read, write, and count are of obvious importance. But how often the simple was converted to the complex! I still can remember such trigonometry equations as sine over cosine equals tangent. I have been out of high school since 1947 and no one has brought it up. Who was first, Magellan or Balboa? How often do we refer, or have need to refer, to the Nina, Pinta and Santa Maria? We were stuffed with data, a good deal of which is of relatively modest value. And whether it is or is not important is aside from the real disservice— that is, that the learning process was so caught up with the absorption of information there was no room left for weaving in the human element. It was mechanical, without warmth or emotion. Through an amoebic motion we gravitated toward seeing complexities where there were and are simplicities.

The complex will not satisfy a prospective buyer. Certainly we deal with complex subjects that are fundamentally emotional as well. But the *conveying* of our message must be one of stark simplicity. If you approach prospects with an array of multisyllabic, unfamiliar terms, thinking you will dazzle them with footwork, you will receive that classic "thousand-foot stare in a ten-foot room."

I have often been misquoted on my assessment of the importance of product knowledge to an agent—which I place at five percent of capabilities. The catch lies in knowing as close to 100 percent of that five percent as you possibly can. Knowledge of people accounts for 95 percent. If you get an A on every exam on product knowledge but know nothing about relating to individuals (in effect, the "high touch"), you will fail.

This leads directly to the initial ice-breaker—and the ensuing financial planning interview—with a prospective client, a referral in all likelihood.

For this occasion, I select breakfast as the best of times. People generally are in neither a good nor bad mood early in the morning. People usually leave home mentally with an empty basket, so to speak, putting in the good, taking out the bad as they navigate through the day. Hence, breakfast is a good time for interviews.

The pleasantness and productivity of the first meeting hinges on your ability to direct the conversation.

CONTROLLING THE INTERVIEWS

The more talkative participant dominates the session; the good listener controls it. Your objective is to control. Get through the amenities, get into some soft questioning, and then get out of the way. Listen.

My traditional opener is to allow to my guest that "You don't know me from Adam, but (mutual acquaintance) seemed to think it would be worthwhile getting together."

No two interviews are ever alike, for no two people are alike.

I never have used the same conversational routine a second time, once the opener is dispensed with. In any case, however, you must rehearse mentally. Motivate yourself to relate to this individual you are meeting for the first time. It is not his or her job to relate to you.

Ask them questions such as, "Do you have a spouse? Children? Really? What do they do?" Keep it as elastic as a rubber band. Drop a question and then tune in.

If you remember throughout the interview that you have only one opportunity to make a good first impression, by the time breakfast is finished, you will have connected with a follow-up nine out of ten times. Actually, during the first ten minutes the buyer decides what to do. You may have difficulty in accepting this because you may have found that it takes you two to three hours to relate to a person on a favorable basis. But, in all honesty, you may also admit that this is an exception. I find that a person accepts or rejects what I have to offer early in the conversation. Remember that the purpose of your first contact is to get along psychologically with your prospect—so that he or she will want to meet with you again.

When it comes to follow-up, I suggest my office at, say, 7 p.m. The prospect is intrigued enough to show up mostly because the breakfast we spent together was lightweight. Contrary to conventional training principles, I make no attempt to bag a lot of information at the first meeting. I am happy if I can work in a few basic references to my financial planning philosophy and see how the prospect relates to it. This tactic demands delicacy and consistency. (To exaggerate— you do not swing from an ultraconservative posture to discussing an investment in oil exploration somewhere off Afghanistan.) When I try to get prospects to discuss investments, I of course do not fail to discuss the importance of continual savings. Above all, I make sure prospects know I care very much about their welfare. It is much more important to show concern for a prospect's future than to appear successful. $400 suits, $200 shoes, $35 ties, and the other trappings of success mean nothing to a prospect. But your obvious concern means *everything*.

The breakfast meeting is casual, loosely structured, free-flowing, and dominated by my guest; but the second is formal and orchestrated—and I am the conductor.

THE EVENING INTERVIEW

Let me set the scene. With me are "Bill" and his wife, "Jenny" (to whom I extended an invitation to attend via Bill). They are parents of four children, aged 9, 11, 13, and 15. Bill is an entrepreneur, aged 40. Income? Be careful when you are seeking this information. *Never* ask, "How much do you make?" That question is not only indelicate—it is inadequate. Discuss "income" information. This information is all-encompassing, and the word has much more appeal. I have never been stonewalled when determining a prospect's "income." All that is required is a little confidence building—then disclosure flows easily.

The same discretion applies to Jenny. To establish whether she has income, I probe with, "Jenny, are you working *outside the home?*" Never imply to someone who may be a housewife and mother that she does not work unless she works at a paying job. As it turns out, Jenny is a full-time mother and housewife. Bill is the sole bread-winner, at $60,000 a year.

To ease them into the second interview (Jenny's first), I categorize the four groups people fall into relative to their finances: the uninformed incompetent, the uninformed competent, the informed incompetent, and the informed competent. I find very few uninformed, incompetent people and, likewise, very few informed, competent people. Most of us are competent in our specific discipline or job but uninformed when it comes to personal finances. For example, take the legions of physicians who are experts at their practice but less than expert beyond their discipline—that is, when it comes to their personal finances.

I *know* that while I am discussing competence, Bill is comparing his financial competence with that of a body of highly intelligent professionals. His eyes tell me that he is conceding he (an educated, intelligent person), too, does not know much about finances. He may even admit this out loud. In any case, his body language has already spoken to the point.

I then hasten to make my own honest admission, which serves to quickly restore Bill's positive self-image while putting us on equal footing in terms of respective professional competence. "Bill, Jenny, there are only two things I know about—money and people. Get me beyond my clearly defined realm and I'm a babe in the woods. But people and their money have been my field of professional study throughout my adult life."

To elaborate, I relate a true story, much to the consternation of a vice president to whom I told it during a speaking engagement in Monte Carlo. It is, simply, that I always carry $2,000 cash on me, especially when I am traveling. When he replied, to my statement: "John, you shouldn't carry all that money; you could be robbed!" My response was, "That's exactly why I carry it. If some man comes up to me and says, give me your money, I'll give him $2,000—and he'll be happy. A happy person won't shoot me." My point is, of course, that I aim to please.

SPENDING AND SAVING

Below are a pair of circles that represent one of the most profound truths in the area of finance. I actually go to a blackboard and draw these two circles for prospects such as Bill and Jenny.

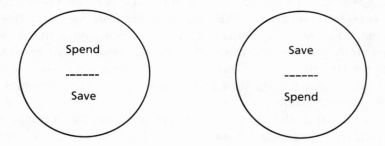

I draw them one at a time, beginning with the left circle, saying that there are only two kinds of people in the world in the area of finance. As I fill in the first circle, I note that there are many who spend, then save what is left. As I go to the circle on the right, I add that there are very few who save and spend what is left over. Then I look at them and say: "Bill and Jenny, you are about to hear the most powerful phrase you will ever encounter in the area of finance." I point to the first circle, noting, "These people always work for (now pointing at the circle to the right) these people." In which circle would they prefer to be? In the right, naturally.

As I draw an X through the left circle, I tell Bill and Jenny about a boyhood chum who was sporting a list of all the kids he could whip in the neighborhood. One of the tough guys of the neighborhood came along and demanded, "Hey, let's see that list." Looking it over, he said, "You got my name on there. You can't whip me!" My friend said, "Fine, I'll scratch your name off." Beats the hell out of fighting.

I now am ready to proceed with the seven-circle diagram I have used at some speaking engagements and seminars but which I have not, until now, described in detail. The diagramming does get a bit convoluted at times, but I think the analysis will meet the standard

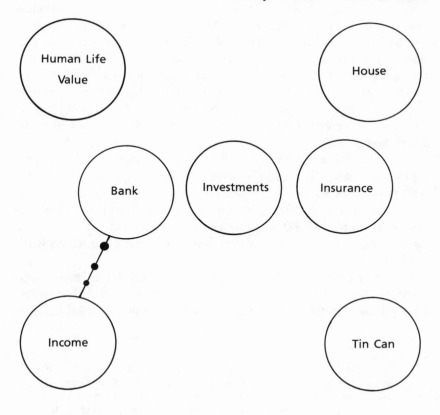

of simplicity I expect—the standard by which we both work confidently and effectively.

I invite Bill and Jenny to join me in studying the circles in order, beginning with "Human Life Value" in the upper left. I explain that, as we place values on material things such as homes and cars, I want them to think about themselves as people, the value they attach to their lives, and what they want or hope to realize from themselves as a family unit. Each of us needs to retreat periodically from the treadmill long enough to consider what we are doing with our lives— and *why*. Encouraging this process is constructive in itself, for it helps the counselor to know his prospect better and it helps build rapport.

Next comes the lower-left circle—"Income"—which obviously must be dealt with before you can proceed with any sensible guidance. If you follow the interviewing pattern I outlined previously to derive this data, you should have no trouble in finding the pertinent amounts of data you require. In Bill's case, for example, the total annual income for the family is $60,000. Using this basic information, I tell Bill and Jenny that by the time we have traveled through the seven circles, they will know everything they will need or want to know about total financial planning—through a process that took me nine years to develop. I also compliment Bill for being among the top five percent of the nation's earners, which makes him and Jenny feel good.

I then discuss each of the three middle circles—"Bank," "Investments," and "Insurance"—which, collectively, account for the whole world of finance as shown on the next page.

I begin with the "Bank" circle on the blackboard, which is then connected to his $60,000 income circle. Between the two are several smaller, interconnected circles signifying the social demands on Bill's pocketbook.

I then comment, "Bill, despite all you may have heard to the contrary from radio, TV, print, or any other form of advertising, your bank* account is the single most important facet of your total financial

---

*By "Bank" I include savings-and-loan institutions. The stress here is on liquidity, ready access—and peace of mind. There is both value and comfort in having available a solid "kitty" to contend with the unexpected but inevitable setback. What about, for example, Individual Re-

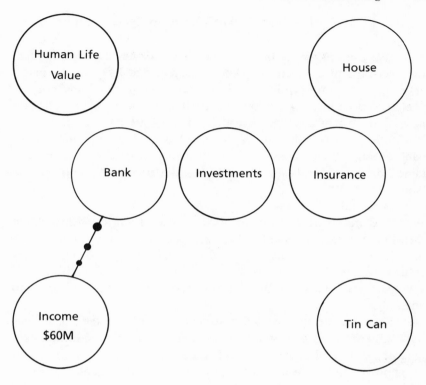

planning portifolio." (Pay special attention to the foregoing para-
graph—I truly believe that the bank account is the most important
facet of financial planning.)

tirement Accounts, with their tax-sheltering advantage and competi-
tively attractive dividends? My answer is that Bill and countless others
in his age group and financial condition are far better off giving top
priority to their bank or S&L account. For all the attractiveness of an
IRA, its payoff without penalty is at age 59½. Early withdrawal also
imposes taxation. Bill may not be able to wait nearly two decades to
tap a reserve.

Conversely, a secure tax-sheltered annuity, with no penalty for withdrawal, can be very advantageous for a depositor at almost any age.
Even without a penalty, however, withdrawal from an annuity carries
with it a tax bite. The tax has already been applied to a bank or savings-
and-loan withdrawal; what you withdraw is all yours, free and clear of
penalty and/or taxation.

THE PLACE OF SAVINGS ACCOUNTS

By stressing Bill's bank account I am distancing myself from the ever-present competition. And because basically I am an insurance agent, I am surprising Bill—pleasantly—for he was not expecting that an insurance seller would relegate insurance to a position inferior to that of a financial institution, i.e., a bank.

I then tell Bill that although I emphasize the importance of his bank account, I also appreciate the difficulty in making regular, sustained deposits. "Bill, how would you like to have $20,000 in the bank?"

"I would."

"Before we go any further, then, I will let you in on this: Most men in a $60,000 income bracket, with a wife and four kids, do *not* have $20,000 in the bank. It's hard to understand the deluge of ads calling on people to take their money and put it into all sorts of savings, when most of them don't have any money to put into anything."

I have made it easy and reasonable for Bill to tell me he has only $3,000 in his bank account. Why did I suggest a $20,000 savings account? I offer no hard and fast recipe. I simply have settled on approximately one-third of total income as a plausible figure all other factors considered.

Once we have established Bill's total income, the fact that he has only $3,000 in his savings account and that he is agreeable to raising that savings figure to $20,000, we move to the second middle circle, "Investments," with its satellite circles. I emphasize there is no hurry for him to get from $3,000 to $20,000. This is an extremely important part of the interview—to get him relaxed.

I will not belabor the "Investments" diagram because it is fairly self-explanatory. You will note that in the circle in the upper right-hand corner is the house, which is not an investment, never was an investment—and never will be. Until a person is willing to sell his or her house and move into, say, an apartment, that money cannot be counted. Be very careful in your explanation of this, for many people believe that their house is an investment. They believe this even though for most people the day of making a lot of money on selling a house, *in my opinion*, has come to a screeching halt.

Bill has a modest pension/profit-sharing plan as an entrepreneur, a cushion that should, he hopes, expand with the anticipated growth of his enterprise. Meanwhile, he cannot afford high risks (no one should ever risk to the tune of more than five percent of his or her estate) and he does not have the leeway to invest in stocks or bonds. For the time being, then, Bill's concentration must remain with circle number one, "Bank," and to a lesser degree with "Investments."

Now, on to the third circle in the middle. This is where the fun really begins as we construct and dismantle "Insurance."

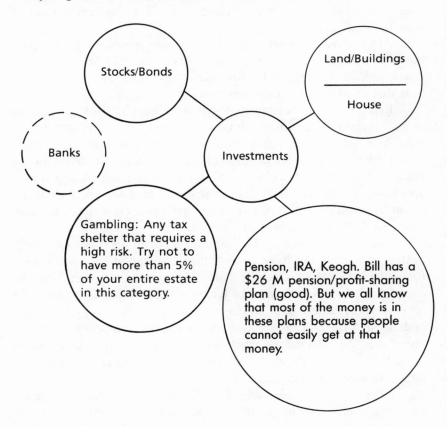

SELLING THE INSURANCE

Anyone who has had the experience of sitting in on an insurance interview will recognize the defense mechanisms that are evident in the prospect. Please understand: Many people do not like insurance; some people do not like *insurance agents*; and in some cases, their feelings may be justified. Now let us circuitously attack this product that we all love.

"Bill, here's one of the most important pieces of financial planning advice I can give you: Insurance is the *least* important facet of your financial plan."

Are you ready for the next move? If your prospect does not pass out with that statement, you certainly have his or her attention. Bill is astounded—he never in his life heard that or ever thought he would hear that from an insurance professional.

It is my strong feeling that it is no longer possible to operate as an insurance *practitioner*, an insurance *agent*, or an insurance *person*. You *must* be a financial planner and you must be totally interested in every facet of your clients' problems in the world of finance. I am not telling you what to do, but I am stating how I operate—and this is exactly *how* I operate. In doing so, I chalk up a win by establishing confidence and trust based on honest candor in what I truly believe to be fact.

I have been "training and explaining" with a prospect, not educating him. I do not have enough time for that. What I make time for is the building of a solid relationship by way of simplifying the complex. I believe that at this juncture I must touch the prospect deeply. The grasp by the human mind of finances is somewhat limited. What I hope to give you is an impressive, intellectual passport into the realm of finance, which will ultimately help you to understand the complexities of this much-discussed subject. My job is to take complex facts and make them simple.

I then examine the materials Bill has brought along at my request (generally, anything pertinent that may shed light on Bill's financial position, e.g., will, trust, passbooks, stocks and bonds data, insurance policies, etc.).

Remember how you were educated and trained in our business? You were told to pick up the person's policies, bring them back to your office, weigh and evaluate them, and state that you would be back in touch in two or three weeks with some insights about what they have and what they should have. But policies are not that complex. There are only three pertinent pages in a life insurance contract—the cover showing the amount, the cash value table, and the application. The rest is boilerplate. Do not try to impress people with your intellectual skills. Be candid, open the contracts, and note the information you want to pass on to them. You can determine the cash value in minutes. The companies make it very easy for you. Most face amounts end in zero, so anyone can determine these amounts.

Bill, it develops, has five policies. In sequence, their cash values are:

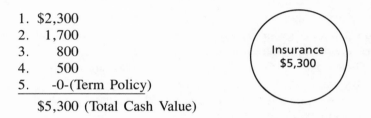

1. $2,300
2.   1,700
3.   800
4.   500
5.   -0-(Term Policy)
    $5,300 (Total Cash Value)

Insurance $5,300

Please remember this is also a savings. If you become a client, sometime in the future I would like to see this cash value reach $20,000.

I then reinforce what I have said: "Bill, as you have heard me say, your savings account is the most important, the urgent element in your financial arsenal. Bright people save before investing."

The stage is now set for the zenith of the interview. All that has preceded this moment pales by comparison.

THE TIN CAN

"Bill, I think you've decided you want to save. But very few people know much about saving so I would like to illustrate by drawing three little saving circles. In one circle I'll put bank account paying eight percent. On the second circle I'll put bank account paying five percent. In the third circle I'll put my beloved tin can."

Then I say, "Bill, if you put $500 a month in the one savings account at eight percent, and you put $500 a month in the one account at five percent and you put $500 in the tin can every month for five years, at the end of five years, where would you have the most money?" Before he can answer, I go on to say, "In the tin can, you're only allowed to put the money in—the top closes and you aren't allowed to touch that money until the end of the five-year period. However, you have open accessibility to the other two vehicles. At the end of five years, where would you have the most money?" And 98 percent of all people say, "In the tin can."

I then continue: "Success or failure of a savings account has nothing to do with the interest. It never has and never will. The success is determined by your deposits. It is determined by a systematic methodology of putting money in—and *keeping* it there. Most savings accounts go up and down, and the fact remains that 90 percent of our society has little money anywhere."

Then I explain to him, "Bill, obviously we are not going to use a real tin can. Life insurance is a tin can."

I now explain that I consider *my* life insurance a consuming, finger-cutting "tin can." And that can—my life insurance policies—now contains $240,000 of cash value.

I tell Bill, et al., that I *love* my life insurance product and that I love the discipline that had to accompany its growth. Pity those who manage to pay their bills but never manage to pay themselves through the calculated process of putting some of their hard-earned money aside where they will not, short of calamity, get their hands on it. To resume:

"Bill, you said you'd really like to have $20,000 in your bank account, right? Right. Do you think you and Jenny can save $1,000 a month?"

"Hell, no!"

"How about $600, then?"

"No way."

"Four hundred, maybe?"

"Well, we'll give $400 a try."

And many people say that. It is not for you to tell your prospect what to save, so this line of questioning allows you to "fail with honor." And I might insert that, *you* have to use *your own* personality in *your* interview.

"Good, Bill, your monthly savings target is $400—or $4,800 a year. Let's say you allot 80 percent of that, or $3,840 to your bank account. With the $3,000 you already have on deposit, added to the new $3,800, your total in a year, excluding interest, will come to more than $6,800. You're taking care of the most important circle." Bill and Jenny exchange satisfied smiles. We're on the way.

THE "LEAST IMPORTANT" CIRCLE

"Now, for the 'least important' circle. Let's say you put the remaining 20 percent of your $400 monthly goal, i.e., $80 a month, or $960 a year, into new life insurance premium. Make sense?" Bill, along with 99 percent of my interviewees will invariably answer, "Yes." Next move.

"Jenny, Bill, you may not agree, but your house was not, is not, and will never be an investment. I know this runs counter to everything you've been programmed to believe."

The disbelief persists, nonetheless. "Try this on for size: You have a $100,000 home, a $42,000 mortgage, and you're paying $600 a month. Bill, if you're going to have money in your home, make sure it's someone else's. Mark me down as Exhibit A. My first house cost $27,000. I sold it for $47,000. My sweet wife, Kate, calculating faster than a state-of-the-art computer, squealed, 'Whoopee, a $20,000 profit!' Not so. We bought a $100,000 replacement—minus the $47,000 from the sale of the previous home, leaving a $53,000 deficit. Add to that my $20,000 'profit' and I'm still in the hole to the tune of $23,000. And that's just for openers. We've added on three times. We now have 17 rooms and four furnaces. My January heating bill was $600. Now, understand, I'm not knocking any of this. A house is a key part of your 'Human Life Value,' one of the seven circles of your total financial plan. My point is that a house is not an investment. Until you can sell it and move into a tent, you cannot count the money on a home."

On to the next item: "Bill, how much insurance are you now carrying on your $100,000 home?"

"One hundred thousand worth."

"Honest? You're kidding." He wasn't kidding. Now let us go over to the Human Life Value circle.

I might say "Bill, if you were never to receive a raise over the next 20 years, you'd be getting $60,000 a year times 20, or $1,200,000. If I said you needed that same amount in life insurance, you wouldn't agree, would you?"

So, for now, I ask, "How about $600,000 worth of life insurance, total, including the $150,000 you already own?"

"Sounds reasonable," they agree.

"I'm going to make it sound even better. You already qualify for $200,000 worth of 'government decreasing term life insurance' by way of Social Security." They smile. "And you have $50,000 worth in Bill's group policy." To recap:

        $600M Life insurance objective
       − 200M Social Security
         400M
       − 150M Insurance owned
         250M
       − 50M Group policy
        $200M To be purchased

After teaching the foregoing, I explain that Bill can obtain the $200,000 insurance coverage balance with the $80 per month he has already committed to apply toward this end. It is simply a matter of selecting appropriate buys from an available mix, spanning ordinary to term to universal life. (More smiles.)

NO FEES

Now, to top it off: "Bill, if you follow the mode we've worked out together; I think you'll have a beautiful system. If you should die, you'll leave your family the amount of money you'd be earning yearly, without their having to touch the principal. And each year you live, your net assets will go up. We'll also be keeping in contact, seeing how you're doing, offering advice where necessary. Unlike others, there's absolutely no fee for my consultation on your total financial planning, now or later. I get paid only from the insurance

premium end of your plan, the least of your savings objective."
(Smiles, smiles, smiles.)

High touch.

Believe me, it works, for my clients and for me. A scant four
failures through all of last year testifies to that assertion. If I knew
an approach that could top it by so much as one sale, I would use
it. But I am satisfied no such plan exists.

We have gone through the paces with the upwardly mobile,
relatively wealthy, 40-year-old entrepreneur/family man. Next, I will
demonstrate how to consult with the young, single person.

THE INTERVIEW WITH THE SINGLE INDIVIDUAL

Personally, I think the young, single man or woman employed
for the first time is the greatest market in the financial planning field.
There are a lot of them. They are fresh entrants. They want things.
They need things. But they have no plan, no pattern for a solid future.
Because we have been around longer, we can readily place ourselves
in their shoes. We have the perspective that allows us to admit that
we probably would do things differently if we were just starting out.
Don't forget that. Keep it prominently in mind when you confer with
them. You were once at that tender age, with all its hopes, aspirations,
fears and naivete. As I have told numerous audiences, my definition
of the perfect appointment is one with a 22-year-old who is fresh
into his or her first job.

Most of my youthful prospects materialize, as do all the others,
through referrals from satisfied clients. And I give them the same
time, interest, and effort I provide to an older wealthy client. First,
they deserve it. Second, many of them will mature to the big leagues
and, if well served, will reward me accordingly. And, third, I really
enjoy helping young people get started on a realistic financial planning track.

At my first get-acquainted session with a young prospect, I have
in mind my three major circles, i.e., "Bank," "Investments," and
"Insurance"; but I employ them with a totally different approach. It
is important for you and your young guest to establish his or her
wants as opposed to his or her needs.

THE IMPORTANCE OF A CAR

Our present example reveals to me that the prospect is a 22-year-old male, a college graduate in his first month at a new job, making the heady sum of $15,000 a year. Our low-key conversation gradually unveils that he is living at home with his parents and is paying them $100 a month for the privilege (others in the same situation will pay varying amounts). He owns a rattletrap automobile with tires that seemingly have to be changed once a month. The car is a constant but necessary evil, never reliable, always a threat of embarrassment or worse. Not at all surprisingly, he discloses that his burning ambition is to own a new car as fast as possible. Here is where I want to caution all would-be successful agents with youthful prospects: Do not try to steer him or her away from that big romance with a new car. At that age, in those circumstances, the urge is as natural as filling a need to eat or sleep. Think back to the time you had a junkyard candidate and could not wait to get rid of it. Remember how you had to deprive yourself and work like a mule to get through school, longing for the day you would be driving around in a new set of wheels, sniffing that new car smell, drawing envious glances. *Agree* with him that it is a solid objective, that it is exactly what you would be shooting for if you were in the same boat. But interweave with your support the prospect's agreement that, despite his nonexistent savings and substantial desire, he wants to establish a long-term savings goal of $10,000—*a must*.

The young people I meet have as much need for financial security and independence as anyone else, but they just have not given any thought to it. If you approach them in a reasonable, relaxed manner and are logical in your thought process, you are going to have an audience.

Now you have the background to fine-tune these ambitions, through a prospect whom you have encouraged in his quest for an automobile and who you find is willing to accept professional advice on what to do with his thousand dollars plus a month take-home pay.

At that income level, I counsel that my prospect should put the least amount possible as a down payment and that he stretch the balance over four years. He agrees on this score as well as on the sensible point that he is not yet ready for a fancy, high-priced car;

a new and modest one will do. He settles on $300 a month for his car. With his $100 outlay for living at home, his needs figure now comes to $400. What to do with the rest? Give him the ball. Let him play around with this question: How much a month do you think you can save *easily*? Almost invariably the answer will come in too high. It's a trade-off, a compensation for spending all that money on a new car. He will want to put in something to balance living it up. He responds with $300 as a savings goal. I always cut it down. I want it to be easy for him to achieve his objective, not have him stretch beyond his ability then soon get discouraged and scrap the whole package. He accepts my figure of $200 for savings, while smiling his appreciation for my understanding and support.

When you are dealing with a young person, keep your ears open and your thinking elastic. Many have had to pay their whole way through college. They may have loans to pay for tuition, car, clothing, and other things. When this is the case, I emphasize what should be the obvious—concentrate the first years' income on cleaning up those bills. After the debts are settled, then it will be possible to develop a savings and financial plan. In the meanwhile, he or she will have more peace of mind because the debts are being paid off regularly.

Remember your job is to set yourself aside from all other agents who may be calling on that individual. Your emphasis has to be on his or her savings, and your focus on savings should stress the bank account.

Now, back to the prospect who agreed on $200 a month for savings. I point out that doing so will put him at his $10,000 passbook target in just four years. He likes what he hears and will undoubtedly follow my advice about a savings account.

The next circle, "Investments," I refer to but do not dwell on. Yes, I concede to him, there is entirely too much media hype on investing. Everybody has got a "hot item" for anyone's available cash. But, realistically, I must advise my new young friend that investments are for the back burner—a subject we can explore fully later on, after he has mastered the initial but vital phases of his financial planning savings. No argument. He accepts the rationale.

Remember that while I am speaking, I am thinking, in the back of my mind, that 80 percent of the savings is going to the bank and only 20 percent of savings is going to go for insurance.

Next on the agenda is the "Insurance" circle. At this stage my young friend would be the rare exception if he were not on guard; he expects me to lay out a hefty package, something that would more than make up for the investments I have just told him he is not ready for.

Surprise! I tell him that insurance is the least important phase of his financial plan, which is what I tell every prospect or client. In his case, insurance is the *least* of the *least important*. I tell him that if he were to insure heavily, he would be denying other, more legitimate needs for the chance that he would die young and leave a big estate for his parents. I tell him that if he marries and begins a family, later on we will review his insurance policy based on his new and more-involved requirements. The big difference, now, in talking to this young, single person is that the 80 percent for the bank account, 20 percent for insurance formula has been changed. Now we will talk about 90 percent of the savings going to the bank and a mere ten percent going into insurance—because, very honestly, he does not need any insurance. Someday he will need it, but right now it is important only to get *something* started at a young age; we will build as the need arises. I do mention a low-cost "guaranteed insurability" rider to hedge future needs. But, for right now, I counsel, he should put 10 percent of his $200 per month "Bank" account figure into insurance, which comes to $20 a month (in no event would I advise him to go over $30 a month).

I DON'T OVERSELL

Some will say I am missing a golden opportunity to put in an apple and get an orchard. But they also miss the whole thrust of my philosophy, which is rooted in the beauty of truth and is nourished by patience and periodic grooming. If I were to sell big right out of the box, I'd be overselling for a need that did not exist. I also would be less inclined to maintain the regular reviews my clients are entitled to that keep us together. When you have annual reviews, you have clients. Furthermore, getting the maximum from a customer, especially a youngster, may soon pit his or her insurance payments against other, more-pressing needs that develop. Instead of being comfortable, he or she will be bothered. And people who are bothered for any length of time will begin to suspect they've been had . . . by you. Then where are you, not only with that person but with the pals who could have been referred by him or her to you? In downplaying insurance, in recommending just $20 a month in premium payments, in emphasizing that a savings goal of $10,000 is attainable in four years, I have brought my young prospect completely into my corner. He knows he will not go broke putting $20 into anything and he will respect my sales restraint and the interest I have in his total financial well-being.

Now that the insurance monthly premium has been determined, I draw a half moon as a discussion aid in describing for my young prospect the kinds and relative values of insurance. Specifically, there are only four questions that you need to answer. How much life insurance should I buy? What kind should I buy? When should I buy? From whom should I buy?

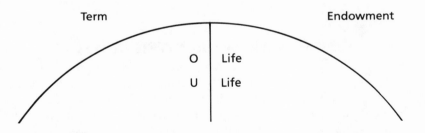

Term   Endowment

O | Life

U | Life

I explain briefly that the younger a person is when buying insurance, the better. Although it represents a small share of his savings, it is nonetheless an attractive part of his financial plan and personal security. I define and distinguish between term and endowment, ordinary and universal life, making sure I avoid the tedium and confusion that can swamp a novice. But I wind up the lesson by recommending a permanent life policy as best for him, with its guaranteed payoff.

To the question of from whom he should buy his insurance, I explain (and always say) that I am not here to promote any specific company; that, unlike the casualty business, with, say, 30 carriers, life insurance involves a high number of close, strong relationships between client, agent, and a solvent and secure home office. This relationship, I believe, can be handled only on a one-to-one basis. I tell him that I do total financial planning for all my clients. I charge no fees, no matter how much time I spend. I am paid through the insurance product, and they can buy the insurance from many different people. Most practitioners will only sell them insurance and will not be interested in the other facets of finance. He sees that as very logical—and I end up with a new client.

If you think my pattern of emphasizing the "least importance" of the insurance aspect entails plenty of interviewing and selling—you get an A-plus and go to the head of the class. The old and threadbare routine of going for the jugular with a skimpy number of interviews, counting on gimmicks and advertising to lure the sheep, will not work. My routine does. My advertising overwhelmingly is by word of mouth. Do the job right, be patient, be flexible—and you will have satisfied customers pointing their relatives and friends right to your door.

THE NEWLYWEDS INTERVIEW

Unlike the young man fresh out of college—who has been through the wringer of learning how to conduct himself in that all-important job interview and still can smile despite a pile of bills because he has found work—the newlyweds of today are comparatively well set. In a word, they have money; not tons of it, but enough to get them off to a good start. At many ethnic weddings it is a happy tradition to give the newlyweds envelopes with cash—and to ante up every time the bride is kissed. But regardless of custom, it long has been my observation that, through showers, receptions, friends, relatives, and parents, young couples today have a nice chunk of money when each says "I do."

When prospecting newlyweds, I always strongly encourage meeting with the pair. I also allow at least 15 minutes to set the stage, allow them to reveal what they want out of their new life together, and let them know I want to help them as much as I can with advice that can influence them and their security as long as they live.

If they have no family budget (often the case), I urge them to construct one, using guidelines instead of exact elements. I tell them that being too precise at the outset is too frustrating; just take it easy, talk budget things over, and work it out together.

If they do not have a will (very often the case), I recommend strongly that they see a lawyer soon and have one drawn up.

The young man is 25, his bride, 22. They both are employed. His income is $19,000 a year, hers is $14,000, for a total of $33,000. They have $6,000 in the bank.

I go to my office blackboard and draw the three main circles.

$25,000

Bank

Investments

Insurance

I allow time for the drawings to sink in, then proceed to explain how I hope to help them.

I point out that the bank account is the most important facet in financial planning, but if they are going to make strides in our capitalistic system, they ultimately must concentrate most of their energy on investments, and that the least important facet of their financial plan is insurance.

This is consistent with every other time I talk about these three circles. However, I make a very salient point. I draw another circle. This circle is different from previous ones. I ask them the name of their family doctor and then I put a large X and write his or her name in it. If they have an obstetrician, I put a large X and write his or her name in it. I ask them the name of their dentist and put a large X and write his or her name in it. Then I ask for the name of their attorney. If they have an attorney, I put a large X and write his or her name in it. Then I say that this is what I find as people go down the road.

They will buy a life insurance policy from one person; they will buy another life insurance policy from another person (I am putting small x's in the diagram at this juncture); they will buy a disability policy from another person; they will purchase a mutual fund from another person; they will buy securities from another person; and they will obtain an annuity from another person. I ask them if there is anything unusual about the diagram. "You have a professional here, a professional here; another here, another there. But in this area, where you are spending more money than all the other areas put together, you *don't* have a professional—and I am applying for the job, the job of financial planner." And I want to tell you, that statement is powerful. It gets their attention.

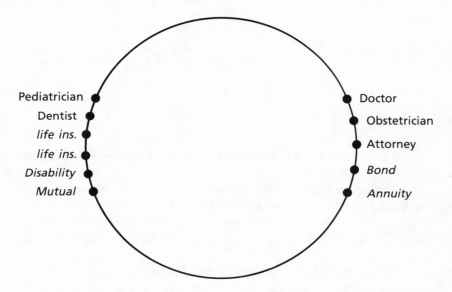

The public is crying out for a professional in the area of financial planning. I explain to these prospects that if I am to assist them fully in this very important arena, I have to know everything about their total finances. I have to know about their income, their savings account, and where they intend to go in the world of finance. Then I ask them, "Does this make sense to you?" They, as everyone, enthusiastically answer, "Yes." I follow up by telling them I am not a family planner, for my field is people and money—but in order to guide them in the latter, I have to know how many people we are going to be dealing with.

In other words, do they plan a large family or a small family? These things have to be incorporated in my planning for them. You would be amazed at how open a young couple will be as long as you are open to them. Once they have told me that they are going to wait a while before having children, I tell them that their job is to put as much into savings as they possibly can in the early years. I will make statements such as, "Put your wife's total income into the bank," which is the most important facet. If they really want to, and they both work for five years with a high degree of discipline, they can save anywhere between $40,000 and $50,000. But even if they fall short, $25,000 is not a bad place to start. So I put on top of the bank circle a figure of $25,000, which represents their goal to put into savings. It does not matter which savings vehicle they choose, whether it be a money market, a cash management account, or passbook savings—so long as they achieve the goal that they find comfortable. And I say to them that if we accomplish this in the next five years, they will be in the upper two percent of society as far as savings goes among young people in their income bracket. They like the sound of that.

My next question is, "What about buying a home?" This is an important question in the interview. Pay very close attention to their reply. You are now into the most precious area of planning for young married couples. *Never* even suggest how much they should pay for a home, where they should buy a home, what neighborhood would be best, or what school system would be best. You are prying into an arena where you have neither the skill nor talent to be successful. They do not need any outside opinion. They will have all they can do to arrive at that answer themselves. When the time comes and they have made the decision of where to buy the home and how much to pay for it, you then can possibly give them some help in finding a good mortgage rate or advising them how to handle their payments—advice within your arena.

In discussing investments, I tell these newlyweds that I would not advise letting their accumulated $25,000, $30,000, $40,000 or $50,000 remain in a savings account. I note, however, that until they have made a decision to purchase a home, they should accumulate dollars as fast as they can—and then make decisions as to investments only after they have bought their home and see how much is left in the savings account. But I would not allow the savings account to erode and then start to talk about investments after the account has decreased $1,000 or $2,000. They should get it back up to $25,000, after they have made a down payment on their home and before they are given any advice on investments.

The first investment they make should be a bond or annuity. You should tiptoe into investments. The way to do so is through a very solid, little-risk position, which both of these vehicles offer.

Just say, for instance, that you have an aggressive young man or woman who wants to dabble in the stock market as soon as the savings hit $25,000. If this be the case, I roll with the tide. I do not believe in trying to play the irresistible force against an immovable object. So I suggest going for the minimum risk, perhaps a high yield utility.

When we advance to the insurance circle, I veer from the path of agents who advocate substantial and equal coverage for both. To me, this does not make much sense in view of the unshakable fact that either could die at any time, without children, leaving a fat bonus to the surviving spouse. Bonuses are nice, to be sure, but in this case the circumstances just do not warrant the extra insurance payment they would have to make, especially when the same money could be put to more productive use. Of course, 10 years later could spell a considerable difference. The man could be drawing $40,000 to $50,000 a year while the woman, who decided to become a home-maker, is earning no salary. At this point, however much insurance is on the new wife would have to be evaluated on the extent of its burden on their total financial plan. My advice is to plan for the worst and hope for the best. You cannot plan for the best and still come up with a good scenario. Always remember that need is predicated on income, and the focus of the insurance should be to protect income and provide security for the spouse and children.

For the present time, I suggest a small life insurance contract on each person, with the amounts adjustable according to such factors as whether the wife remains employed after having children and how much she earns. I then draw two "buckets."

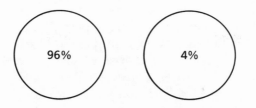

I write "96%" in one circle and "4%" in the other circle. I use this now in about every selling interview that I have. I ask which of the two they would prefer to be in charge of if they had to make a decision to handle 96 percent or four percent of their income. They agree that they would like to be in charge of the 96 percent circle. I then ask: "Could we say that if you do very well with handling the 96 percent of your income, that you really don't care what happens to four percent of your income?" They all answer in the affirmative again. Then I say to them, "I would like to put you in charge of the 96 percent circle, which represents 96 percent of your income. I would like to be put in charge of the four percent of your income," which is the maximum premium that my client should put away for insurance. I will help them with their circle if they will help me with my circle. And I guarantee that at least the four percent I am in charge of will never, ever lose money.

I say to them, "Let's break down your income. You are making $33,000 a year, so four percent would be $1,320 per year. Three percent would represent $990 per year and two percent would represent $660 dollars per year." Here is the powerful part of the interview. Instead of asking them to put four percent of their income to pay insurance premiums, I ask them to start with only two percent. In other words, I draw two new circles and write "98%" in one and "2%" in the other.

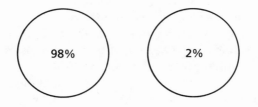

In recommending that only half of four percent of this newly married couple's income be put into insurance, I create a tremendous relief on their part. I am giving them positive reinforcement of my credibility by stressing the conservative side of realism. In their minds, they are seeing me as a buyer *for* them, not a seller *to* them. As they do better, they will reward me accordingly. I then add this powerful phrase: "When you are young, I will take care of you; and when you become highly successful, you will take care of me."

The next question is, "Who should have more life insurance coverage?" Ninety-nine percent of newlyweds will agree that the husband should have more coverage, because they feel that his income must be consistent throughout their married life. Let the couple dictate the division. Do not step in and tell them that all coverage should be on the husband, and none on the wife, or 50-50.

The dollar that we are going to spend for the coverage has been arrived at quite easily. In this process, with this routine, you will build lifetime relationships.

Because I have treated this young couple as the very important people they are, either one may wind up at the top of their fields, spawning greater involvement as clients themselves and sparking as many as 50 new renewals to my office.

Insurance sales have entered a new era and the formation of a new family unit offers exceptional opportunities and challenges to the professional planner who can keep pace.

I cannot predict accurately that this couple will end up making $200,000 a year or $80,000 a year or $50,000—or whether they will become executives or social workers for the rest of their lives. I can predict, however, that those who do extremely well will stay with you and you will be paid handsomely for serving them in a client/agent relationship. Remember, too, to offer the same service to those who do not become financially successful. The poorer the income, the more help they will need. You must serve all.

Before I move on from our newlyweds, I am going to comb through the awesome importance of trust. As an insurance representative you are building a relationship of trust. Once violated, you have nothing. It cannot be bought for any amount of money—it must be built carefully and slowly. You have to demonstrate, start to finish, that you are dedicated to helping and protecting your client—that you are his or her friend, indeed and in need.

It is your business to sell, but the first thing you sell is yourself. People do not buy insurance or financial planning. People buy *people*. Selling is convincing your prospects or clients that you know what is best for them. To do this properly, you have to know them better than their own families know them, better than they know themselves. You have to know their needs, ambitions, prospects, growth potential, and risk factors. You must appreciate that you are in a unique, privileged position to delicately extract this data. The more you know, the greater your ability to advise and to reveal your concern and expertise. You will be thought of as a caring, knowledgeable person, and you cannot act that out. If your caring is not genuine and based on personal and professional commitment, your clients and you will lose out. Play it straight; straight is the only way to go.

6

The Professional Prospect

This discussion is necessarily lengthy, for it goes with the complexity of the prospect. The professional prospect I am about to use as an example is a surgeon, one of 186 professionals I serve. (I expect this total to expand significantly. Yours should, too.) Professionals are cropping up like dandelions in summer. The computer phenomenon, for one, has produced armies of designers, programmers, and salespersons where none previously existed. Explosions in franchises of all kinds are raising hordes of managers. Add to this the young professionals who are consultants after they have been with a major corporation for just a few years. You could work this market alone and be busy eight hours a day.

My doctor prospect is 48, has a wife and five children—one in college, two in high school, and two in grade school. Just because he is a doctor does not mean he is making a lot of money and worth a lot. I compare physicians to the hen, the ostrich, and the eagle: Hens fly low and heavy; the ostrich never gets off the ground; and the eagle soars. Doctors encompass a wide field, financially speaking, from the very wealthy heart surgeon to the harried and generally underpaid pediatrician. Some are "fat," others are "lean." There is no rule of thumb. But many of these bright people have in common a stunning inability to handle their incomes. One of the difficulties physicians have is that they are an easy target for a fast-talking sales-man. Add this to the fact that they are not business people and it becomes clear that I have an obligation to see as many of them as I possibly can and give them some tender loving care.

THE CASE OF DR. STEVE

Enter Dr. Steve, who has an annual income of $200,000. I draw my seven circles on my office blackboard, writing down his income. Unlike some of the other prospects, I tell him that at his level I would like to see him with a bank account of $50,000—before he even tells me what he has on deposit. I gear my figure to what he is making and the size of his family responsibilities. I then explain to him that I like to write my figures before he gives me any information so that I cannot be influenced to change my information based on his input. I tell him his bank account, passbook, CD, or any similar savings resource is the most important part of his portfolio. Thereafter, I tell him that once the $50,000 mark is reached, the bulk should go into investments. I practice this preaching, for 90 percent of my money goes into investments.

It becomes clear that Dr. Steve has a way to go. He has $20,000 in the bank and acknowledges he would like to have the $50,000 I suggested earlier. He adds that he has other valuables, including a $300,000 home, a $110,000 sailboat, two Cadillacs for his wife and himself, and two cars for the children. I write down his home as outside his financial circle. Continuing, Steve relates that he owns no other land or buildings, has no bonds, but does have $12,000 in stocks—and a major tax problem.

Last year he paid the IRS $50,000. By the way, the boat costs him $700 a month. Insurance? He has made six purchases from four different agents, revealing he is tied to no one. The policies' total cash value, I quickly determine, is $27,000.

"All right," I say, "this is the third most important day of your life, after being born and getting married. I think you're going to rate this extremely high because I honestly want to help you. But first there are a few things I want to get out on the table. I do a total job of financial planning. I will visit with you every year if you become a client of mine and I will spend a minimum of one hour per year reviewing your situation. I am always available in case you have a problem and you can call and get in touch with me any time from September to May. And, most important, I do not charge. You will never get a fee from me for the work. The only way I will get paid is if you decide to buy insurance and you buy it from me. Let me explain that. You will buy insurance from someone and most of those people will only sell you insurance. But I'd give you free financial planning advice." He fully realizes that I have to earn a living and accepts that as being more than fair.

I go to the blackboard to draw the following:

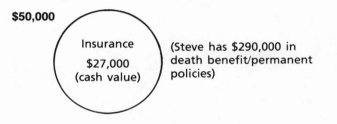

$50,000

Insurance
$27,000
(cash value)

(Steve has $290,000 in death benefit/permanent policies)

I next explain to Steve the difference between a savings account and insurance and between eight and five percent interest (mentioned earlier). Then I bring up the "tin can," which, as you read earlier, concludes that the difference between a savings account and insurance is not three percent but zero and that life insurance is similar to the tin can, with its discipline of forced savings.

I ask Steve, "Would you like to see your bank account climb?" He nods.

HOW MUCH CAN YOU SAVE?

Then I ask the powerful question: "Can you save $2,000 a month?" And he says, "Absolutely not!" Well, I knew that he was going to say that; I always know the answer to each question I ask. Then I ask, "How about $1,500?" Again the stop sign comes up. "Well, how about $1,000 a month?" He responds, as do most people, "Well, we have to start somewhere. Let's start with $1,000."

Good. We have established a savings position of $1,000 per month, 80 percent of which goes right into the bank, the most important slot. With what he has already saved ($20,000), I tell Steve that in about three years, his $800 per month deposits will top the $50,000 mark.

We continue. The remaining 20 percent ($200 a month) is to be slotted for the least important factor, insurance. The insurance has $27,000 in cash value and the bank account has $20,000 in savings. The value of Steve's existing policies will continue to increase—I do not try to destroy what he has already saved. I think many practitioners try to take all existing cash from other policies and build their own nest. However, my job is to serve, not be served. I do not have to make a living off my fellow agents.

I reassure Dr. Steve that we will establish his plan with a three-year program. In two years he will have paid off his sailboat. Meanwhile, it is time to tighten the belt and get on with the strategy, incorporating a high degree of discipline, so that we can arrive at $50,000 in the bank and $50,000 in insurance. I tell him I do not care how long it takes to get the insurance to $50,000, but there is a sense of urgency to get his bank account at $50,000. Understandably, leaving $50,000 in the bank may add somewhat to his estate tax problem. However, I have found that with some degree of liquidity, there is a certain amount of emotional stability and economic security that is established, in spite of the additional income taxes due.

Dr. Steve's house carries a $100,000 mortgage that is costing Steve $800 a month, not an uncommon situation. I ask him how much insurance he has on his home. His answer: $300,000. Again, this is not an uncommon response. I ask him, "Are you kidding?" He says, "No, why do you ask?" At this juncture I move over to the upper left-hand side to the "Human Life Value" circle. I ask him, "If your income remained the same over the next 15 years, how much would your human life value be?" Well, obviously it would be $200,000 times 15 years, which is $3,000,000. "Steve," I continue, "you've insured your home for more than its value. What if I asked you to buy $3,000,000 worth of life insurance? You would say I needed a psychiatrist. But you have a house that will probably survive both of us and the next generation and you have it fully insured. If I told you you needed $3,000,000 in coverage I should be committed.

But I just wanted to give you a comparison. Is it asking you too much to insure half of your human life value?"

Steve's response? "You mean buy $1,500,000 of life insurance?" And I say, "No." And the reason I say no is that he responded very negatively to the $1,500,000 figure. "We don't need that. I see you already own $290,000 worth of coverage. So you only need $1,210,000 worth of coverage." We lightly banter back and forth. He asks, "Do you mean buy $1,210,000 worth of life insurance?" And I say no because of the tone of his question. I add, "Steve, Social Security will give you the equivalent of about $500,000 worth of life insurance of a decreasing term nature. So you only need approximately $750,000 worth of coverage." Understand that in the interview the client is not looking for an exactness but rather an approximation, especially when we talk of Social Security. We would have to have supernatural insights to look ahead and see what Social Security is going to give us down the road. Do not try to be too exact with your client. Draw a big picture—but draw one that honestly reflects your best evaluation.

This is the honest thing to do, for your client will grasp the fact and appreciate the validity and integrity of your analysis. I say, "Steve, if we have an additional $750,000 coverage, it is all you are ever going to need. We must satisfy the protection and then later make some adjustments. The reason you will never need any additional coverage is that your pension and profit-sharing and other investments will increase as your income increases. But let's fix the amount even if it's all in term insurance coverage." Do not be afraid to sell a lot of term insurance. In effect, it is your arsenal. It represents an inventory for future business when it ultimately will be converted.

I have stated to Dr. Steve that he will need a trust. He will wonder what the advantage would be. I tell him it will do a great deal, noting that we will analyze his profit-sharing/pension plan in a separate meeting.

THE ESTATE PLAN

As for a trust, I explain to Dr. Steve that if he were to die in two or three years, his wife would benefit from an unlimited marital deduction and his $1,500,000 estate would be tax free. But what if there were a simultaneous disaster, that is, both Dr. Steve and his wife perished at the same time? It is a possibility, I tell him—and he agrees—but it also raises inheritance complications that no lay-person can handle comfortably—hence the need for a lawyer to pre-pare a trust, to sensibly arrange distribution of the estate in a prudent manner.

I briefly suggest an even split between wife and children, al-locating $750,000 to either side. Some, of course, would argue that the wife should receive less and the children more because her death would create an exemption on her amount. I believe in the even division, for "balance," as well as for the interest that will be gen-erated from either side's $750,000 inheritance. Steve agrees. I offer to arrange a meeting with a bank trust officer or attorney to handle the particulars. He readily accepts. Note: I have kept clear of his expensive boat and two expensive cars, which he obviously feels strongly about. In not doing so, I have fashioned a bonus for myself in his appraisal.*

It is, I tell him, a "can't miss position." He is delighted. His confidence in me shoots up the ladder. I do not hurt myself, either, by convincing Steve of the need for an expert's look at his disability coverage. I am not the expert, so I refer him to one in my office who does have such expertise. My colleague keeps abreast of all trends in disability insurance particulars. I make the referrals, he does the work, and there is a commission-sharing arrangement. I think this is fair. Never be afraid to bring in others to handle complexities be-yond your competence. Do not be parsimonious in rewarding such assistance, either. Your colleague also has to make a living and feel he or she is being dealt with fairly and equitably.

---

*In looking at Dr. Steve's financial situation, I also find that the net proceeds of his profit-sharing/pension plan are closer to eight percent or several percentage points below what he could otherwise be realizing. I recommend he invest $50,000 in a 12 percent annuity that, I tell him, will be worth $100,000 in six to seven years (as of this writing). I find it a very good vehicle to get some secure, limited, downside-risk in-vestments. I believe strongly in annuities and they have in the past few years become a big part of my portfolio.

With the professional prospect there is no trickery; you do not have to have the pen ready or the application out. The professional will agree with the need if you have done a good job of selling, and often I put all term insurance coverage on a new professional because I want to ease into an agent/client relationship. This case might result in total term insurance 80 percent of the time.

WRAPPING UP THE SALE

To wrap things up, I call in my secretary to handle the paperwork associated with Steve's personal medical background and arrangements for a physical. I also excuse myself from this meeting for approximately 10 minutes, to cultivate the feeling within this client that I do not tune in on anything in his personal life more than is necessary to help him create a total financial plan.

When I return for the handshake and goodbye (indicating that there will be an annual plan review), I ask how Dr. Steve would prefer to begin payment for his $200 per month insurance. It is a very casual inquiry without any hint of pressure. The usual reaction is to pull out a checkbook and pay now. If he would rather send it in within a few days, my demeanor tells him that is fine with me— and it is. *Hard-selling at a close is a killer*.

While everything is fresh in mind, I ask my secretary to type a summary one or two pages long on the main elements of my new client's plan. This will form the basis for the annual review. The essentials are that Dr. Steve will deposit $800 per month in the bank, which, after a year, will show a total of $30,000, including what is already deposited. He will have $200,000 in investments (with no new stocks, bonds, or "gambling") and $35,000 in life insurance cash value.

THE ANNUAL REVIEW

This part of my program is probably the most rewarding, both psychologically and financially. I told Dr. Steve I would sit down and meet with him once a year and now I have followed through. So a greater trust exists when he comes in to see me. Moreover, I know that he will not take care of many years of "sinning" with one year of penance. He is there.

"John," Dr. Steve gushes when he sits down for his first-year checkup, "you won't believe what happened." I listen.

The good news is that his income has grown to $250,000. And you and I both know that the $200 a month he paid for insurance— or $100 a month or $300 a month or $50 a month—has always been paid, thanks totally to the tin can discipline imposed through our first meeting.

The bad news is what he was in charge of. He is a candidate for president of "Spenders Anonymous."

Dr. Steve's bank book showed $23,000, a paltry $3,000 more than he had a year ago and $7,000 below the target. (His interest alone would have accounted for $2,000 of the skimpy increase!) Instead of $800 per month in bank deposits, he had managed only $100. Regrettably, Steve's performance is not out of the ordinary for an initial try at fiscal solvency; rather, he is all too normal. Still, he is embarrassed.

I do my best to allay it. I want to help him, and the first step on the road to helping him "dry out" is to listen sympathetically and give him time to mumble that he wants to give it one more try. After all, if he were totally unashamed and unrepentant, he could have passed up the appointment. That he did come back was all the evidence I needed that he could still be salvageable and that he considered me a trustworthy means to that end.

The second annual review reveals an encouraging turnaround. Dr. Steve's home mortgage has dipped a little, to $94,000. His profit-sharing/pension account, with earned interest and deposits, is up to $261,000. The bank account shows $42,000, both cars are paid for, and so is the boat. A conversion has taken place.

At the end of three years, Dr. Steve's passbook contains $60,000. Here, I tell him, is where he really can start blossoming.

First, he buys a $25,000 municipal bond at eight percent, which adds $2,000 annually in tax-free income. Next, I enlist $25,000 from him for a commercial real estate deal I put together for myself and nine other partners— with me, as always, the biggest single investor, i.e., the greatest risk taker.*

The resultant write-off trims Dr. Steve's IRS bite by a tidy $11,000 and he has a triple-A tenant, to boot.

If half of the coverage Dr. Steve has bought was term and half was ordinary, I will convert a little bit of the term to ordinary from year to year. I will sell $200,000 worth of term insurance on his wife and Steve will subsequently convert the balance of his term to permanent. That helps me in *my* income; it complements the whole picture and, of course, keeps me totally in touch with my client. At $4,800 a year for insurance, his renewal account at five percent brings me $240 a year, nice payment for annual reviews.

In six years, Steve and his wife can survey:

Pension/Profit Sharing	$500,000
Bond Portfolio	50,000
Real Estate	25,000
Stocks	25,000

THE PLAN WORKS

In a nutshell, Dr. Steve, who actually began with me a number of years ago, is within striking distance of $700,000 in net worth, at the comfortable age of 55. I provided the time and advice. He provided the dollars and the determination. It worked and it still is working. Dr. Steve has since sent me three more clients. More recently, I have had him take much greater leaps into real estate, for the tremendous write-offs they offer, and to take some modest gambles with $10,000 in silver and the same amount in rare coins. I refer

---

*I have been managing such ventures for years, for what now totals 150 partners. They are superb and honest tax shelters. I have never lost a dime on one and neither have my partners.

my clients to the experts, who get the commissions. I believe in doing a good job for my customers, not in raking in everything I can lay my hands on.*

I invested a total of ten hours in Dr. Steve, and my secretary invested another ten. From this I derived, with first-year commission and renewals, more than $2,000. And it will continue to come in, because my staff and I are efficient and effective. No time is lost conjuring up elaborate proposals. I propose as my prospect's story unfolds. As one decision is reached, we move into another element in his or her financial plan, always remembering that efficient people do things right—and effective people do the right things right.

Frequently, colleagues confront me with the objection, "But, John, you have more *time* than I have." My retort is to ask to see the person's watch. "Funny," I say, "but you seem to have the same number of hours that I have." The point is to make the best use of it.

Let me digress briefly to glance at some areas I have not yet covered.

Dr. Steve, for example, was overspending. While he was not about to relinquish his possessions, he was mindful of the need to change for the better. He straightened out when I brought home to him an awareness of income versus savings.

You are bound to run into prospects in name only—the type who want to live it up, who do not think insurance is worth their time, who figure they will die relatively young, but who will probably survive into their 70s or 80s. You are wrong if you think you can sell these people.

THE GRAYING MARKET

Conversely, compared with the occasional person who will not give a serious thought to tomorrow, there are countless people in their

---

*When it comes to socializing, I should note that I don't mix with Dr. Steve or virtually any of my other clients. My role is to serve as their financial planner. My family consumes virtually all my free hours.

50s who are apprehensive about the future. They represent one of the most dramatic attitudinal shifts I have ever seen. They worry about Social Security and whether it will still be there when they retire. Teachers with their own retirement program fret about the possibility of it being commingled with Social Security—and diminished in the process.

There is evidently increased concern among wives about their situation after their husbands die. In the past decade, they have come to realize to a chilling degree that they are favored to outlive their spouses by six years or longer. So, it is only natural that many of them want their husbands to maintain their life insurance until death—permanent versus term. The same principle applies in one respect to those who retire prior to 65. Although they have the right to convert policies, they see the cost as prohibitive and still too costly even with a partial conversion. This is the reason people should get their permanent insurance coverage purchased before age 60.

I always advocate permanent coverage; it always pays off. I have spent nearly three-and-one-half decades in the business, yet only 19 of my clients have died. Life insurance is one of the few solid institutions in the world. It is an industry well-entitled to take a deep bow and receive a big pat on the back.

7

The Business Person as a Prospect

The "Business Person Interview," in my opinion, offers the most interesting possibilities in financial planning/life insurance selling. Within limits, that is: I have chosen to prospect among entrepreneurs and small- to medium-size company business people. Very few of my clients work with major corporations and I have not one major corporation as a corporate client. The big employers have held out bountiful security blankets to their employees in the form of benefit packages. Many of these employees "bought" their respective large corporations for life. Most believe they have adequate coverage and look forward to a comfortable retirement, protected from all perils. So they buy expensive homes, join clubs, enroll their children in exclusive schools—everything but save money. Too bad so many corporations of late do not return the same degree of loyalty. Thousands of "lifetime" employees have been cut adrift with half a paddle in a very choppy creek.

THE ENTREPRENEUR

The entrepreneur, on the other hand, is a completely different breed. He or she does not have built-in security, no group insurance or disability coverage at the outset—plus, he or she works 12 or more hours a day. Busy or bored, the entrepreneur will welcome financial planning on my terms, with a breakfast meeting followed by a later session at my office. Moreover, you and I are entrepreneurs, which makes for a nice understanding when we get together with a hard-driving counterpart. Much the same can be said for the small- to mid-size business person.

My example of the latter begins by virtue of a referral from a satisfied client who suggested to his friend Jim that "John would be a good guy to get with." We agree to meet for breakfast at one of the three restaurants I always use for a morning rendezvous.

I want good food, good service, and an atmosphere that will not make us feel rushed if the conversation extends longer than an hour.

The term I want to introduce here is "mental rehearsal." From the time I wake until I drive to the restaurant, I rehearse mentally how to converse with my prospect. I remind myself that there is only one chance to make a good first impression. I need to keep the chatter light the first two minutes or so, while waiting for the order to be taken. We need to get to know each other as individuals. I should not pry about who handles his group or life insurance, investments, etc. I should use as a conversation springboard a few bits of infor-mation about him I picked up from the referral source and tell him a bit about myself. I must not pitch or even *mention* insurance.

Breakfast usually arrives within moments of the order. And it is finished faster than other meals. By the time the dishes are cleared, I have determined the sequence for observations I will make to whet Jim's financial planning appetite and influence him to make a follow-up appointment at my office. I tell him I have been offering total financial planning for a quarter-century and that, among the numer-ous things I tell my clients, I advise them on how to cut down on their taxes.

A light goes on. Have you ever come across a person who thought he or she was paying too *little* in taxes?

I also let many of my prospects know that their child's college education can be tax deductible. Another light goes on.

Once the dishes have been cleared, I flip over the place mat and start some circle doodling:

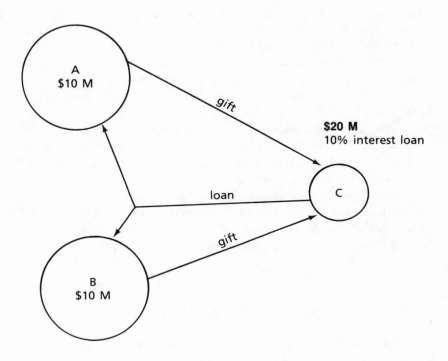

I draw three circles: (A) including $10,000 and put an "M" for mom; (B) $10,000, dad; (C) Another circle—child. A and B give $10,000 each to the child. That's allowed under the gift tax law. The child then loans the $20,000 back to the parents and charges them ten percent interest. Obviously, there then is a $2,000 interest paid from the parents to the child.

There is nothing wrong with that. You can pay interest in advance. It is deductible. The child gets the money tax free because of a lower tax bracket and then takes it to his local college or state institution that pays his education. If you do that for two years in a row, you're receiving $4,000 and you pay their college education, deductible for the parents, tax free to the child.

Once I have done this, I mention another service, that of accepting invitations to go to business establishments to give talks on motivation or financial planning for their employees. The workers appreciate the attention and it is free to the employer. Jim may not say anything to this but his expression is a sure tip-off that he is thinking about applying it to his shop.*

"Jim," I continue, "I can't tell you how many times I've heard proud business people tell me they're making the greatest thing since sliced bread. But when it comes to their personal planning, something's lacking. They have no will, no trust, no personal financial plan. They see an attorney only when they have a specific problem. Their accountants stick to numbers and steer clear of personal aspects of financial planning. And by and large, most business people don't get around to grooming a successor."

Throughout this little monologue, Jim is nodding in agreement. He becomes more interested when I admit I have bought and sold 20 companies for my clients. I calculate that Jim is an avid fan of at least four of the subject areas I have addressed.

"HOW ARE YOU PAID?"

But then Jim asks a question I have vowed not to broach in our first meeting: "John, if you do all of these things, how are you paid?"

"Very simple, Jim," I respond. "I do plenty of personal consulting and I give a lot of talks for the likes of McDonald's (the fast-food folks) and The Andersons (a large Midwest partnership in grain and retailing) and never charge a fee for the time and recommendations. The *only* thing I expect is that if a client elects to buy life insurance as needed, it is bought from me. And I say to myself, so long as they are going to buy, why not from John Savage?"

Jim and practically everyone else I have explained this policy

---

*Speaking at a business gets results. Former Dana Corporation Chairman and CEO Rene McPherson introduced me to then-President Stan Gustafson—now deceased—with whom I spent several hours, after which I was invited to give a series of lectures to his employees. Although I did so without charge, it led to a fair amount of subsequent business with Dana employees. It is a highly positive form of p.r. that can pay handsome indirect dividends.

to agree it is an eminently good one. To those who may feel I am shortchanging myself, I wholeheartedly disagree. I am not partial toward jumping over dollars to look for pennies. Besides, doing it my way keeps me a free spirit. I know of no more productive approach, no better bottom line for the time I invest.

Jim is anxious for the follow-up meeting at my place and agrees to bring all of his important pertinent papers, savings account statements, and net worth statements. By now we are talking quite candidly.

He arrives on schedule three weeks later, understanding we are having lunch in my office. If a prospect is really interested that prospect will come—and during the day. As for lunch, I keep it simple. We dine on cheeseburgers, french fries, and sodas, delivered in ten minutes by my secretary, at a cost of roughly $6.00.

Once we have eaten, Jim gives me a picture of his total net worth. It appears as though he has all his eggs in one basket.

A SUBSTANTIAL PROSPECT

Jim's vital statistics: age 47, wife, three kids (high school); company valued at $1.6 million; $8,000 in the bank; no stocks, bonds, buildings, or tax shelters; $80,000 per year income; $50,000 in group life insurance, with between 50 and 70 employees. Jim personally bought five life insurance policies with a death benefit of $230,000 and a $2,000-a-month disability policy. Jim owns all the company's stock; he is the president, his wife is vice president and treasurer (he did not want to bring her along to our meeting!). Many of my clients prefer not to have their wives at meetings, but some do; I accept their desires.

Jim's will is 15 years old and has never been reviewed. He has two cars owned by the company, a $300,000 home virtually free of debt, and no boat or club memberships.

Jim does not exactly hate insurance people, but he does not have his office walls lined with pictures of them either. Maybe he thinks he has been had or has come close to being had by an agent. I do not know or care. All I know at this point is that Jim cannot have come at a more opportune time. Not for my sake—for his. In about 24 areas Jim urgently needs the kind of help I can provide. By sticking to the provision of help for him, first and foremost, I know I will eventually find he is taking care of me.

Jim's purchase of five life insurance policies from four different agents signals to me that he is tied to no one. I think his $50,000 group policy is ludicrous, but he is comfortable with it and that will do for now. Having all his money tied up in his company is, I believe, dangerous. But that is the way he wants it. He wanted his house paid off and he paid it off. It gave him some peace of mind, an advantage that cannot be ignored.

Jim needs help but in order to accept it he has to have some careful guidance. Where to begin? He goes along readily with my suggestion for an update on his will and admits that a trust could have some distinct advantages. I have now told Jim that we will separate his planning into two categories, personal and business. He is content with this and my first recommendation.

I draw the seven circles on the blackboard. My main thought is to get him into a tax shelter. Jim's worth is roughly in excess of $2,000,000.

"TALK TO ME IN SHORT SENTENCES"

Jim does not need to be hit over the head when I tell him about the pitfalls in his will and how his estate would be much more secure with a trust. Obviously, he will need professional assistance, so I volunteer to submit to him the names of some competent lawyers from whom he can choose. Jim waves me off with, "John, save me the time and just go ahead and pick one." His comment reminds me of a story told to me by an old friend, Jim Murtaugh, who heads a local die-casting company. He had been going into a rather long-winded description, supposedly for the benefit of a top executive, when he was suddenly cut short with the admonition, "Talk to me in short sentences." The executive, just as my client Jim, was a busy man who wanted to cut through technicalities and get to work. He wanted concise descriptions and crisp recommendations, not a dissertation. Good lesson to keep in mind.

Small-to medium-business people may not have the imposing degrees of their big corporate counterparts, but they generally are intelligent and preoccupied with getting things done *now*. Do not burden them with nonessentials. The "smaller fry" may have to scramble hard, but they also have the keen satisfaction of feeling they have a better grasp on their own destinies. If they have a solid financial plan they no doubt are correct in their appraisal.

WRAPPING UP THE SALE

I lined up Jim with an attorney and they worked up a solid A.B. trust. Jim also agrees with me that he should add $700,000 of life insurance on a split-dollar basis (his corporation pays the premium). The corporation is in great shape, he is using corporate vehicles for personal trips, and the insurance angle seems a natural.

Next, we draft an employment agreement funded to the tune of $500,000 in life insurance with the corporation as owner and beneficiary. I sell a new group insurance plan and, in the process, increase it. I also sell Jim an additional $4,000 a month in disability income coverage. Along the way I conduct a financial planning seminar for Jim's employees (no fee) and reap five new clients. The pension/profit-sharing plan is added to company benefits. There are no life insurance sales for me in this, but it is one of a number of welcome suggestions that cement a probable lifelong relationship.

My total commission for doing business with Jim is in excess of $5,000—this on the strength of four meetings. With the annual reviews, new and different sales opportunities will arise. Meanwhile, my income per year from Jim over the next decade will range between $500 and a $1,000. This is very nice pay for the services I rendered.

I am convinced that if you devote time and expertise to the type of business people I have been describing—if you learn how you can help them the best you can—you will find yourself busy every hour of every day. You will grow vertically with what I consider to be one of the hottest market prospects in the country—hottest because it is virtually untapped.

I told you earlier I have bought/sold 20 companies for my clients. Here is an approach I have used successfully on five occasions. Keep it in mind. Perhaps the right opportunity to use it once will surface—and make your year. Here is the background and the strategy:

A SALABLE IDEA

Joe is 60, his wife, 57. They make $50,000 from a little business they built together in a small rural town. It is part—a big part—of their lives. To them, it would be salable only if they went with the sale. And they are not really all that interested in a sales proposition because they figure they will just work until they die.

I ask Joe: "What about a buyer after you die?" Joe says, "Sure, it'd be great for the family, but the place wouldn't be worth much without me."

"O.K., Joe—if you wanted to sell it tomorrow, what price would you want?"

Joe estimates $300,000.

I then suggest that he buy a $300,000 life insurance policy, with the company the buyer and owner. If he dies, his wife gets the going price for the company and still has the company.

As I said, I have parlayed this approach to good effect five times. Tuck it away.

8

Understanding
and Balance

People who want to succeed in sales or in anything else, for that matter—have to get off the treadmill long enough to consider what makes them tick, how they communicate, and why they think the way they do. In this chapter I will deal a bit with the process of becoming more self-aware. What I will describe is based on scientific analysis, as well as the thoughtful rummaging of philosophers. I also will incorporate my own observations—as neither scientist nor philosopher.

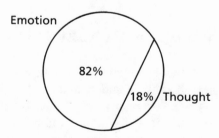

The diagram above represesnts what I believe to be an approximate chemical division of the human brain. Roughly 82 percent of the human brain is related and responds to emotion. The far smaller share, 18 percent, is devoted to thought. I often jokingly refer that "this is why there is not a great amount of thinking going on."

Some of the world's greatest thinkers, including Plato, Aristotle, and Socrates, agreed that there is a recognizable order, a ranking, in the thinking process. From the most important to the least important step, the sequence is as follows:

> Understanding
>
> Wisdom
>
> Prudence
> ———————
> Mathematics
>
> Memory

Understanding, wisdom, and prudence require progressively higher levels of intelligence—the ultimate is the ability to understand.

On the other hand, below the line are math and memory, indicating that a person can excel in either and have a low intelligence quotient. Morons have been known to memorize sequentially the numbers on a train of box cars or display extraordinary abilities in computing math problems. But they do not have the ability to exhibit prudence. According to St. Thomas Aquinas and Emmanuel Kant, to be prudent is to be above average in brainpower. But to be merely prudent can mean living essentially as an automaton, making sharp distinctions (life is either black or white) and feeling very duty bound.

WE DO NOT UNDERSTAND

I think one of the most awesome deficiencies in the human being, the greatest of beings, is understanding. People do not attempt to get in sync with one other on a regular basis. The consequences range from the extremes of war, murder, and assault to the relatively lesser but still terribly important areas of mental abuse, misinterpretation, abrasiveness between management and labor, and inability to sell a product.

Schools generally do not provide much help in enhancing understanding. Although an occasional talented and caring teacher may help a student's communication skills, formal higher education in interpersonal communication and understanding is confined mostly to a few passes at sociology, or perhaps a course in basic human psychology. When it comes to dealing with people—spouse, children, colleagues, prospects, clients—most learn by trial-and-error. This lack of skill in interpersonal communications is reflected in the enormous sales of materials meant to provide those skills. In actuality, communicating effectively means nothing more than having the intelligence and capacity to understand.

I have an uncomfortable suspicion that our lack of understanding is getting worse, not better. No longer is there an interplay among people so necessary to finding out how others live, think, and react. Thus, people compound the problem of understanding by compartmentalizing lifestyles, limiting thoughts to shrinking mental ghettos— and dutifully passing along this dubious tradition to the children.

GROWING UP IN TOLEDO

As a child, I was fortunate when it came to trying to absorb the understanding of others. I had six sisters and two brothers who *had* to understand each other and work together because there was no other option. My mother died when my brother Bob was born and my dad had no patience for a house divided.

Working at my father's store (which all of us did) was like getting a Ph.D. in understanding. Ours was a rough neighborhood and I learned very early how to fend for myself.* The many wonderful people in my neighborhood also helped me mature.

I learned from my father the equally important skill of making my intentions understood. Sassy children were lifted by my father,

---

*Comedian and former Toledoan Danny Thomas described his old stomping ground as a place where the guys hit a passer-by over the head with shovels and bet pennies on which way he'd fall. The center of Danny's turf was about a half mile away from mine. When the toughest of his neighbors felt up to it, they'd throw caution to the winds and move to my neighborhood just to see how long they could survive.

pinned to the wall, and told in 150 decibel language that they would be ground sausage if they were ever caught mouthing off like that again. My father did not have the time to learn all the subtle nuances of child behavior—of understanding the children who occasionally annoyed him—but he had no trouble in making *them* understand *him*.

The lessons in understanding people continued uninterrupted from the store to the parochial school I attended. I had the good fortune to attend a school that had a healthy mix of ethnic groups. Many children were very poor and from broken homes. Others were from middle-income families and were fortunate enough to have good parental guidance. Many lived the straight and narrow and others the not-so-straight and narrow.

THE START OF HIGH TOUCH

Some might call what I acquired in the way of understanding through childhood "street smarts." But I do not think the term applies in my case—for what I assimilated was "high touch." Through self-discipline, a respect for adults, and exposure to a variety of people, I achieved "high touch" and a high degree of balance—which are the bedrock of my personal and professional life.

THINKERS VS. DOERS

When it comes to mental reactions, I believe people fall into one of two slots: those who are thinkers and those who act (thinking people or action people). Because of their intelligence and ability, thinkers can learn or be taught to be action people. But doers, who lack innate skills, cannot learn to be high-level thinkers.

Thinkers who also want to be doers need to ensure their attitude is positive. Fortunately, over the past 12 years much more attention has been paid to promoting positive attitudes. I am pleased by this trend because I am convinced it can cause good thinkers to become doers.

I believe that *intelligence* means being quick to apprehend or grasp an idea, as distinct from *intellectual ability*, which is the capacity to *act wisely* on what has been apprehended or grasped. A person may possess a good mind but be uneducated and unable to communicate effectively: "I know what I want to say, but I just can't seem to be able to put it into words." This person is a thinker who cannot act. But with some coaching—teaching—this person can learn to act, to communicate.

The salesperson who is all "do" but no "think" is, just as Willy Loman, the main character in "Death of a Salesman," living professionally on borrowed time. Prospects may like the hale-fellow-well-met, but that hale-fellow will not get their business on personality alone. The salesperson has to deliver and delivering consists of guidance based on knowledge and understanding—knowledge of knowing every facet of the trade and understanding every facet of the prospect and client.

Today's professional has to think, learn, do, and tell in order to win. This means having a keen sensitivity to every word coming from a client's or prospect's mouth.

Recently I was one of a three-member panel at a seminar for insurance agents in Toledo. One of the agents asked us how much of our work was divided between time with our prospects/clients and time on back-up, planning, etc. One panelist answered that ten percent went toward prospecting and/or contacting clients. The other said 25 percent. But I said that I spend 80 percent of my day with customers or prospects. I do not think it necessary to devote so much time to back-up and paper-shuffling—especially considering all the sophisticated office equipment now available. I think too many agents fritter away precious hours playing with numbers, trying to cram all buyers through the same hole when there is no single pattern for all.

By seeing more people I sharpen my skills proportionately. Consider golfer Jack Nicklaus. Although he has natural abilities, he has been hitting golf balls longer than anyone else on the pro tour. Any normal, healthy person who hits balls eight hours a day, year after year, will become a good golfer.

THE GREAT MOTIVATOR

While I am considered a motivator focusing on how people think or fall short on thinking and doing, I would like to touch on a related and common failure: the stubborn refusal to accept or hit the truth head on. In various lectures, I have told my audience that the most important motivator for salespeople is *money*—that nothing happens until a sale is made (which is why salespeople earn and deserve the most). Teachers who listen to my talks usually are aghast at so crass a materialistic line. What about security and recognition?

I give them my priorities—

1 Money

2 Security

3 Recognition

—and then I tell them the following:

Ten years ago I brought into my office a young trainee at $10,000 dollars a year. He did a good job. Two years later he had security and an annual paycheck of $14,000. The next year, at 24, he was at $20,000. I called him into my office, congratulated him effusively, and told him I would run a full-page feature ad in the local newspaper (of him and his wife) in recognition of his doing the best job ever for a 24-year-old.

He was out of the chair, beaming. Then I added that there was just one other thing I had to say—I was cutting his pay in half. The young man's drained face told me I could stick his recognition in my ear. He preferred a paycheck to the recognition.

The teachers to whom I have told this story understand why salespeople rank money so highly.

If you train or manage salespeople, you need to stress the importance of the trainee's productivity—for productivity will escalate *income*, the paramount consideration. Everything else comes after it. Whether it be for a home, food, grass seed, or a shovel, people need *money*. And at the same time, a salesperson needs balance—nothing in excess. Balance is the product of emotional stability and economic security—and neither can be achieved without an adequate income.

I think one of the best examples of people who have achieved balance is the new entrepreneurial trend in the People's Republic of China. After years of looking down on capitalism, they are starting to incorporate aspects of it. A farmer, for example, who overproduces can now peddle the surplus and keep the proceeds.

I sincerely believe that this trend will pave the way for peaceful coexistence. Contented people do not want to see their lives evaporate in a mushroom cloud. It is the malcontents who see no other solution to their problems than to slug it out in war. But communication and balance make for contentment—and peace.

9

The Road to Excellence

As is the pathway of life, the road to excellence is always under construction. Sharp curves, soft shoulders, pot-holes, and ditches call for keeping eyes peeled, paying full attention and steering determinedly toward the objective of successful selling.

For a long time I have tried to be lead dog of the team. The lead dog is the only dog that gets a change of scenery. I think it is worth bearing in mind that, unlike humans, lead dogs and their followers have the innate sense to avoid falling into ditches. Although it can happen under bizarre circumstances, generally, dog teams have an admirable capacity to stay afoot. Unfortunately for a lot of us higher animals, going over the edge—after flirting with it on and off—seems almost habitual.

Several phenomena seem to account for this quirky human tendency to gum up an otherwise solid chance for success and happiness. For example, Soviet antagonism in the 1950s, combined with their feat of lobbing a rocket into space, catapulted the United States into an agonizing academic reappraisal. Almost immediately, the United States, heretofore a country only mediocre in science and math, became a nation of science/math experts. Money by the billions was requisitioned for space achievement and the educational foundations for that achievement—so much so that a youthful President John F.

Kennedy could predict confidently (and all believed) that the world soon would see a man on the moon.

But while we gloried in our achievements in space and in the technological growth they spawned, it became increasingly clear that we had been throwing the baby out with the bath-water. Our national commitment was lopsided; while we indulged science and math, we shortchanged crucial social and communications skills. Our families were being split by divorce. The odds of a marriage lasting decreased significantly. And the emotional battering of parents and kids was (and is) beyond calculation.

Similarly the United States can boast of young high school and college graduates who can calculate brilliantly but who cannot function when it comes to comprehending an article, enunciating their thoughts with any degree of coherence, or writing an understandable letter. I would like you to always keep the following in the back of your mind. No matter how well we accelerate technologically, we cannot afford to erode new relationships.

THE NEED TO UNDERSTAND

In broad terms, then, I believe our current and future national road to excellence must be repaired and resurfaced by an infusion of marriage instruction and greater concentration of communicative skills in our schools. And we have no time to lose. Because without family stability, there can be no personal stability, which is the essence of success in anything. And if we cannot converse accurately and efficiently, we will become a motley mixture of peoples with different languages and cultures—and nothing is more conducive to friction and misunderstandings than a multiplicity of tongues. Instead of cohesiveness we will have more small, narrowminded enclaves.

I am not minimizing the importance of science and math. Competence in both is necessary for reasons of competition and national security. What I am pleading for is a tolerable trade-off, to give communicating and marriage instruction (which, incidentally, go hand-in-hand) a break in our high school classrooms.

Perhaps, in crying for educational reform, I am like Don

Quixote, jousting with windmills. Yet, I still believe George Bernard Shaw, who wrote: "Some think of things that are and wonder why. I dream of things that never were and ask, why not?"

Conversely, no one can wait around for change, educationally or otherwise. We are on the road. The question is, is it the road to excellence? Ultimately, each person has to judge for himself or herself the destination and speed on that road. I would like to offer some leads to help you along the way.

I remember an answer James J. Corbett gave to an admirer who marveled at how this remarkable heavyweight boxing champion could absorb so much punishment and then go on to win. In those early days of pugilism, it was not uncommon for two opponents to batter and pummel each other for the better part of a day. The fight ended when one was either knocked out completely or could not stand and make it to the middle of the ring. Corbett considered the inquiry about his phenomenal staying power, then answered, "I just keep telling myself I only have one more round to go." Think of "Gentleman Jim" when you have taken some sharp blows and wonder how long you can last. Think of going just one more round. Please don't worry about facing a few tough situations. Remember the eagle soars against the wind, not with the wind.

THE "HANDICAPABLES"

Not too long ago, a young Canadian friend of mine was recognized as a champion athlete. At the age of three she had fallen from her father's tractor, losing two legs and an arm at the elbow. I suspect that, at that point, I would have called it quits. Not Roseanne LaFlemme. She just went out and shifted her concentration from one level of athletics to another. In time, with fortitude, she became Canada's Special Olympics high-board diving champion *and* discus champion. Imagine the gutsiness it required to climb that diving board ladder, take the plunge, then do it all over again, time after time after time—to say nothing of trying to balance yourself and throw a discus in Roseanne's circumstances.

On my home turf the fifth graders of Anthony Wayne School

District annually conduct a week-long event to sensitize the children to the problems, concerns, and unique abilities of people who have suffered severe injuries or birth defects. It could have been called "Handicapped Week." Much more accurately, it is referred to as "Handi*capable* Week." Roseanne exemplifies the reason for that informed distinction.

What I am focusing on is the fundamental value in finding sources for self-renewal and self-motivation. Just as we need to guard against slumps and work our way out of them as quickly as possible, we also need to keep encouraging ourselves in order to traverse inevitable bumps in the road. Never ride along thinking you can plow ahead without recharging your battery and fine-tuning your psyche. Broaden your reading. Look for legitimate inspiration.

I caution you, however. Be careful of the authors to whom you are giving your very valuable time. Try to check into their background and what they really know about what they are saying. If they have never been in the trenches (of whatever "war"), they may not have the knowledge that goes with real hand-to-hand combat. There are some clay feet attached to folks who may have many thinking they are something substantially more than they actually are. Do not be tight with your admiration—just realistic.

Oftentimes, we do not know until a real stunner comes along what is going on under the other person's skin. Which brings to mind the following from the pen of Edward Arlington Robinson (a passage I've long since committed to memory): "Whenever Richard Corey went downtown, we people on the pavement looked at him: He was a gentleman from sole to crown, clean favored and imperially slim. And he was always quietly arrayed, And he was always human when he talked; But still he fluttered pulses when he said, 'Good morning,' and he glittered when he walked. And he was rich—yes, richer than a king—and admirably schooled in every grace: in fine, We thought that he was everything to make us wish that we were in his place. So on we worked, and waited for the light, and went without the meat, and cursed the bread; And Richard Corey, one calm summer night, went home and put a bullet through his head."

Extreme, maybe, but not all that uncommon. How often have you been shocked by the announcement a "perfect" marriage was ending, by learning a respected public figure was on the take, or by finding out good, old, easygoing Charley is really a bundle of frustrated knots? People are complex creatures. First impressions are important for setting the stages of a relationship. But they cannot reveal the depths inside. So, while being outgoing, reserve judgment until you feel you really have had the chance to assess an individual. Putting yourself in the other person's shoes can help in this process.

DEALING WITH CRITICISM

I recall the times I was able to watch live one of my favorite football teams, the Dallas Cowboys. During one of these stints, Cowboy's quarterback Danny White practically could do nothing right in the eyes of the fans. They even booed when he felt his jaw to see if it had just been broken. I really felt for him, especially after seeing up close the fleet, mean monsters who were constantly trying to sack Danny into an early grave. I would have loved to have had access to a public address system when the leather-lungs were complaining, to announce the following: "Hey, you on the aisle in Row Ten, Section K; suit up, you're going in for White." In other words, do unto others as you would have others do unto you.

The famous Mexican bullfighter, Domingus Ortez, put it in good perspective when he observed: "Bullfight critics ranked in rows, crowd the enormous plaza full. But there is only one who knows, and that's the one who fights the bull." It's a brilliant spin-off commentary on this Golden Rule.

Adverse criticism is usually an oral assault. It can make one feel down for a while. But if an individual knows his or her own worth, the naggers will not prevail. The history of big shots and little shots is peppered with comebacks against even the most vocal criticism. Abraham Lincoln was a political loser throughout his adult life—until he orated himself into the highest office in the nation—and is now revered as one of our greatest presidents. Harry Truman rebounded with a "Give 'Em Hell" campaign that dumped Tom Dewey, who had been proclaimed unbeatable. Critics supposedly buried Orville and Wilbur Wright under the dictum that people were not meant to fly (and much of that fire and brimstone came from their own father). At one time it was seriously proposed that the U.S. Patent Office be closed because, allegedly, everything worth inventing had already been invented.

Be a fighter in the poetic sense of that word. Hang in there. Repeat the child's admonition that "sticks and stones may break my bones but words can never harm me." Granted, slander and libel can wrongfully damage your reputation. But the sticks-and-stones message is the product of common sense. Remember it—as well as those who have survived and gone on to greater achievements despite critical bombardments.

THE FOUR As

To surmount these obstacles on your road to excellence—and sales productivity—you should display what I call the Four As: Attitude, Amiability, Availability, and Ability. Let us examine these one by one.

Attitude. A positive attitude is an important quality. In our business, we are surrounded by so much negativism that it is imperative that *we* be positive. It is necessary for our own mental well-being and it is important for the effect that it has on our clients. We are the ones who have to set the tone for the quality of the contact. Who wants to do business—or even pass the time of day—with a sourpuss? Please remember that a negative thought is a down payment on an obligation to fail.

We can influence—no, *change*—our state of mind by thinking positive thoughts. We influence what our brain processes every second. If we feed it optimism, we will be optimistic. If we feed it cheerful thoughts, we will be cheerful. If we give it enthusiastic thoughts, we will be enthusiastic.

Is attitude important? How can you live with yourself—how can others live with you—if your attitude is not the best?

Amiability. To me, this means being friendly, upbeat, fun to be around. If your attitude is great, you will find yourself being pretty amiable, too. One follows the other. Being amiable means that people will look foward to your visit or phone call. You will be the bright spot in their day. And we cannot overlook a basic truism—more people will buy from you if they like *you* (as well as liking your ideas). When the chips are down, the sale is made because of their feelings toward you.

Availability. How many times have you made a purchase—a substantial one—from a salesperson who virtually smothered you with attention during the sales—but when service was necessary on the item, you could not get the time of day from the salesperson? It may have been an automobile or a computer. One day, it did not function as well as it should and you went back to the "dealer." If you were told that service was not his problem (but it certainly was yours), how did you feel about this sudden lack of feeling on his part? How did you feel about being shifted off to the "service department"? And what do you think the odds are on your going back to the seller in the future to buy another of his products?

In short, when your client needs you, be there! If more time is needed than was scheduled, give it without checking your watch every few minutes. And if the client wants to talk, *you* talk to the client. The client does not want to talk to your secretary—or the claims office—or even the home office. The client wants to talk to *you*. Be available. If you are, the next time that person wants to buy insurance, it will be from you, not someone else. Please take this final line on availability to heart. Always be available and always say yes.

Ability. This means maximizing, sharpening, and extending the talents you were born with. Even many of our states recognize this need through their continuing education requirements. You will recall that I have said that times are not just changing—they have changed! Yesterday's knowledge will not work today. Even if you are a CLU, when did you take your last exam? Have you looked into ChFC—or CFP? How about the American College's Masters Program? How about teaching LUTC? You never really know a subject until you have taught it. We are similar to athletes because we have to continually "work out" to maintain a level of proficiency. If we let our mental abilities wane, we soon will be out of shape.

LIKE WHAT YOU HAVE TO DO

Do not do what you like to do, like what you have to do. One of the most productive ways of liking what you have to do is tackling the big problems first. Ducking or putting off the serious challenges is a down payment on irritability at best and chaos at worst.

Possibly the most self-destructive forms of procrastination for a salesperson is stalling on arranging head-to-head contacts with prospects.

Recently I spent five hours on a car trip with a young man who is employed as a salesperson by a local company I serve in a variety of capacities. I took the young fellow along as a courtesy and as a way of paying my dues to those who had and have been my mentors. He was good company throughout the ride, listening for long stretches and then tossing in his own observations. A week or so later his supervisor told me his youthful worker claimed it was the most instructive session of his career.

This was gratifying, of course; everyone likes to feel he or she has some teaching abilities. Nevertheless, I was somewhat taken aback—yet greatly impressed—by a follow-up conversation I had with my young driving companion.

The concern arose after I had asked him his preferred times for meeting new prospects. He answered, "at breakfast or lunch"—but then he admitted he had not had such a breakfast or lunch in the preceding week and a half. I admire the youngster for being so honest; he could have lied and told me anything on that score and I would have believed him. Nevertheless, I felt sad about his failure to master his fear and get cracking on what he knew and believed to be the correct regimen. He was afraid of "No." He had yet to realize that "words can never harm me." He had been virtually programmed for failure. In three years with his company, his sales training consisted of gleaning through books and periodicals. He had received no one-on-one, on-the-job training—when he needed at least 50 hours his first year. He had no more chance to overcome sales hurdles than I have of swimming the English Channel with a Doberman on my back.

THE NEED FOR GOOD TRAINING

If you are in this kind of no-win situation, take this book, underline the following comment, and slip it (anonymously, if you prefer) to your boss, sales manager, or whomever: The ultimate in training is on-the-job training. Any company looking for sales excellence *must* individualize its training program so that a trainee receives from 50 to 100 hours of individualized training his or her first year.

I include in the above advice my strong belief that one-on-one training can *effectively* involve the teaching of "street smarts," assuming the *teacher* has the proper background and experience for such instruction and possesses the high degree of caring needed to nurture a trainee. If not—then heaven help that company.

My evidence for teacher-transferral of street smarts (relaying tricks of the trade, passing along tips to reduce blows from the "School of Hard Knocks," etc.) is the entrepreneur. Often he or she has an achiever's background, climbed the corporate ladder, became tired of executive-level pussyfooting, and decided it was time to march to a personal drummer. Almost invariably the entrepreneur who flies the coop does not do so alone. A potentially good helper is enticed to join in on the venture. The potential turns to reality when the helper is coached by the leader into functioning successfully for the good of their mutual cause. They are in the trenches together, one concentrating intently on how the other is doing, learning by perspiration, perseverance, productivity, and pugnacity.

Frankly, I believe that street smarts are learnable, given a resolute, dedicated teacher. Salesmanship is learnable, given a resolute teacher. Unfortunately, U.S. colleges and universities train students in almost everything *but* salesmanship. We are shortchanging young aspirants to business careers in the most crucial aspect of their college education. I am reinforced in this belief by the dozens of letters I have received the past year during lectures in which I have criticized our business colleges' sales-training deficiencies. There remains a great gap between education and the companies that employ the educated—so much so that I believe the first university or college that comes up with a graduate or undergraduate degree in *sales* will reap a dramatic increase in enrollment—and American business will heartily applaud the long-needed innovation.

10

Building an Agency

I realize that if I am to write a book about selling, I must include the subject of this chapter, i.e., building an agency and the management that runs it.

Let me play devil's advocate for a few moments. Let me begin by saying that I might want to treat such a subject "under protest." And let me say that I know a person who sells insurance cannot be accused of being completely unbiased when he writes about management. Some emotion may surface in the following paragraphs and some comments may be irritating to the manager or company official who reads them. Let me soften all this by saying that yes, I realize we all are in this together—agent and manager (and home office). Of course, we are. And yes, I know agents need management—and obviously management needs agents. So much for the givens. Now let me rattle the bars of a few cages if I may.

From my window, the world of management sometimes comes across as mediocre. I wonder if some managers believe that they are managers simply because they have been exposed to management theory at institutions of higher learning. I also wonder if they could be deficient in the much-needed practice and experience of being effective teachers—and leaders.

I am not against colleges. I think the product they turn out is fine in many cases. But as I have already said, selling is something different. College is great for helping to show how to live by introducing history, science, the arts, language, and so on. And in many courses, students frequently can get solid hands-on experience as a springboard to their careers—for example, in the classes where they work with computers, or in media centers where they can operate cameras, write scripts, and edit video tape.

But you will look long and hard to find anything remotely comparable in college for would-be sellers—or managers of sellers. If the schools are not taking this seriously, what effect does it have on us—the people who sell life insurance? To answer that, let me give you a very strange scenario, one you are not likely to see.

Assume that to become a doctor, you do not have to go to medical school. Oh, yes, you are encouraged to study biology, English literature, and so forth to make you a well-rounded person, but if you want to become a doctor, you simply will be recruited by someone already practicing as a doctor and he or she will "train" you. If a particular doctor happens to be a very successful practitioner, she may have left the ranks of actual practice and may now be spending the entire time recruiting, selecting, and training future "doctors." You see, this doctor did so well as a doctor that she was "promoted" to a medical manager.

I will drop this crazy comparison right here. Of course that is not how we produce doctors or lawyers or nurses or astronomers. But it is how we produce life insurance agents or financial planners.

Let me shift gears. We not only have to make better and better products, we have to have people who can sell better and are taught to sell better. No sale, no profit—regardless of how good the product may be.

I think it will be necessary to revamp some of those vulnerable theories I mentioned earlier, beginning with the tattered assumption that the "highest educated" among us should always be the ones in the top management positions. I have no problems with a highly educated person being in top management, so long as that person qualifies for the job in a number of other ways: experience, ability, knowledge, and high touch, among other qualities. But if the "highest educated" standard remains as the sole criterion for selecting the managers, we may have as much chance of changing (that is, improving) our present position as I do of breaking a four-minute mile.

The best managers I have met are those who grew up within

their companies and who earned the total trust and respect of their colleagues as they climbed the ladder—not by where and how long they went to school and the grades they received. Competence, respect, and trust are earned by the individual; they are not awarded to that person after a specific course of study.

Another theory that disturbs me is the one that holds that the best salesmen in an organization should be moved into sales management. That is akin to saying the leading hitter in the ball club should move into management when he retires. It does not work that way. I believe you will find that in sports the best coaches were only average players who had to work hard even to make the team. This gives them the advantage of having empathy for their young charges who are struggling to make it. The player who was a superstar generally cannot understand why someone else cannot do the same thing he or she did.

In our profession, we sometimes have a unique situation: the tendency to take someone who was a failure in selling and to "promote" him to manager. Although today's economics seems to be doing away with this, there still seems to remain a flavor of "if he can't succeed in sales, we'll put him in management." These people may have pleasant personalities, but it is questionable to put them in charge of others who are responsible for making sales. Instead of rewarding failure, we should first seek the cause and then try to remedy it. We should not try to "save" the individual if the solution affects the careers of others who deserve better.

If you doubt what I am saying about insurance company management, I suggest you glimpse at the mail I have received from every part of the country. You manage things. You lead people.

LACK OF DIRECTION

The gist of these letters is that many agents have no one to go to for direction or coaching because their unit manager or general agent is simply not equipped to offer leadership. I love insurance and I am willing to recommend a thorough investigation by home offices to see why our serious managerial problems are allowed to exist.

In order to effect positive change, people must become aware of the degeneration of management throughout the system. Even though the problems are recognized, the "solutions" are questionable.

Raiding parties are sent forth with juicy contracts to lure away successful general agents or managers. Although I have no difficulty with this—not in a free enterprise society—I consider a steady practice of raiding as a flirtation with economic suicide. Raiders can be raided. Loyalty is a commodity that cannot be bought.

Just for your own entertainment, check out the top 100 life insurance companies in the United States and their productivity by agency. You may be surprised to discover that 80 percent of the business is being produced by 20 percent of the agencies. But it does not have to be this way.

Candor prods me to acknowledge that 90 percent of the work performed by home offices on a day-to-day basis is done very well. But there still remains the cloud hovering over the training management of these very same companies. Is training the toughest area? Absolutely! And it will not be remedied by outdated methodology.

The solution according to John Savage? I am being honest when I say I can write 100 positive pages on how to build a successful organization. But I do not have room for all that in this book, so I will limit myself to some pages I believe home offices can take in the spirit with which they are written.

Begin with selection. Every organization or division is nothing more than the lengthened shadow of one person—its leader. As I examine the need, the acceptable candidate for management in life insurance should (1) be successful in sales and (2) have a great desire to build an organization.

But these characteristics are only for openers. A leader has to have the prerequisite skills for the task and, most importantly, a high degree of integrity. He or she also must be a caring individual who teaches effectively by instructing with empathy toward subordinates, especially those who are struggling. Anyone in sales is going to have ups and downs. That goes with the territory. The professional manager/teacher has to be able to spot the downs and move sympathetically to erase them. When an agent is up, it is equally important to share in the joy. When down, understand; when up, celebrate.

COACHES ARE GOOD PROSPECTS

Where do you find people with the potential to direct and bring along winners? My overwhelming preference is for the successful coach-teacher at every level of education. They are *positive*. They are *intensely observant*, able to spot and correct errors. They *want to win* and have the *intelligence* to know they cannot win without teamwork, talent, and dedication. They have *charisma*, that nebulous but vital ability to attract solid people and to bring them along at an individualized pace.

Unhappily for these coaches and the young people to whom they give so much, their financial rewards are very meager when measured against their talents. Good as they may be, they eventually realize they will not have the income of a Bear Bryant. Eventually most of them are prime prospects for recruitment into our profession. I have found that many take to our profession naturally.

When I was building my agency, I had a fairly good idea of the potential of a young trainee moving into management. It was as though the young man wore a label proclaiming it. As soon as he began producing well, I always tried to broaden his duties and ease him into management responsibilities.*

After you select an individual, how should the trainee be trained? Back at my office all five members of the management team are qualifying members of the Million Dollar Round Table. That is, I believe that a *person chosen for management has to be able to make a living selling life insurance*. He or she must not need management compensation to feed a family or make house payments. A productive agent may have no desire to be an administrator. Fair enough; he or she should never be coerced or prodded. Desire is too critical a factor to be compromised. The person aspiring to manage must want badly to train other members of the squad.

Over the years I have encouraged four of our staff to leave and

---

*I have to confess that although I have enlisted a number of young women for my office, I have not yet brought one into management. For now, it is just the way things have gone, which is not to say that picture could not change—and undoubtedly will.

set up their own organizations. I had that goal of establishing my own agency, of leading my own charge. When the urge hits one of my colleagues, I understand and will help as much as I can. Frustration can spoil both barrels, your colleague's and yours. (I should add that my friendly "defectors" went with companies other than Columbus Mutual.)

I take frank pride in knowing that office management teams are the spawning pond for general agents, managers, and home office executives. A young man I trained, Paul Amato, left my management group three years ago and is now vice president in charge of agencies at the Columbus Mutual home office. And he is doing a great job, so much so that I am confident he one day will be the president of a life insurance company.

My pleasure in seeing the progress of Paul and others of his ability hearkens back to the common denominator for solid teachers: They are happy, not bitter, when their students reach greater heights than they have attained.

Thomas Jefferson referred to George Wythe as his mentor. I honestly believe Wythe derived more thrills from Jefferson's enormous accomplishments than did Jefferson himself. I suspect the same could be said about Enrico Caruso's teacher, Ted Williams's batting coach and Wayne Gretzky's junior hockey coach. Great trainers, every one. If only we could begin to train the trainers in our business! I can only hope that what I am writing here will positively influence companies that truly desire change for effective management.

I now would like to look at the high posts in management, the general agent and the manager in a managerial system.

I think the general agent has the best of all worlds. It is an enjoyable job. It is possible to be the leader and still be part agent, trainer, and administrator. I believe it is entirely possible to perform all three of these tasks well and comfortably manage ten agents. There does not exist a company that would not like to develop ten new agencies of ten agents each in the next five years. And if any company has accomplished such a feat, I would love to hear about it— I would lead a standing ovation.

AGENCY LEADERSHIP

When the organization has grown to more than ten agents, it is necessary to add management help to accommodate growth. And this is when trouble can arise. The slippage begins when the general agent cannot bring himself or herself to part with some of the override he or she sees from his or her agents. But the person who does not want to pay for management help—or who pays poorly—will get results more costly than the cost of compensation.

Anyone not willing to share the pie fairly should give up any notions about agency leadership. Good people have to be well compensated if they are to be happy. Only happy people can create the happy environment needed for real productivity. The latter is the whole point in having agency leadership.

This is why I plead with all companies using the manager system of management: *Please* allow—encourage, require—your managers to sell life insurance. They will remain sharp and much more aware of constant changes in the marketplace. They will then become better teachers, because they will be leading by example.

How much training should one expect following selection? I think this depends on one's goals, which I split into three tracks:

Short-term—Six months

Intermediate—One year

Long-term—Three years

To train properly, there must be guidelines, adhered to strictly. The training process breaks down if there is no structure—all too common the case today. There may be mountains of charts, graphs, books, and class exams—but molehills of direction. Too much of our industry's training "regimen" is left to happenstance.

In a trainee's introduction to the first six months, everything expected of him or her should be spelled out in exact detail—as well as everything he or she should expect from the trainer. For the most part, this is not being done. Current successes are more a product of good luck than management guidance. But supervision is a daily routine and the supervisor who does not mandate accountability is not managing properly.

Trainees do not fail by themselves. Frequently, their failure is aided by general agents or managers who were wearing blinders during the recruiting interview or who nodded off in their training and supervisory exercises. If company compensation to general agents and managers were awarded on the success ratio of the trainees, I believe there would be better leadership, better trainees—and much better productivity.

VALID GOALS

Only two things are worth mentioning in goal-setting for trainees. These are numbers of lives and premiums. (There used to be a third, volume, which no longer is an accurate gauge for success or failure.) If I were to emphasize either, it would be number of lives. For a one-year intermediate goal, I would set a target of 100. I would not recommend dismissal for a total of, say, 84. But if the production were fewer than 50, I think the young person should be guided to another profession. If this were the rule instead of the exception, we would break loose from the rut our industry has been stuck in over the past century. As recently as ten years ago, agents at seminars were being drilled with the credo of making ten calls, getting three interviews, and winding up with one sale. My system operates on the *objectives* of ten calls, ten interviews, ten sales. (Again, this works for me, but I cannot recommend these numbers to all, especially newer agents.)

I caution anyone aiming for management at the agency level to first, be sure his or her personal production is providing a nice living—and second, be sure he or she really wants to help others achieve high productivity.

MANAGEMENT STYLES

See how you measure up in this, my four-way split of manager personalities:

Begin with the *control*-type manager. This person is a dictator, who tries to convince everyone that his or her way is the only way. They do not want input from any subordinate or assistant.

The *withdrawal* manager saunters into an agency meeting and lays down the guidelines for precise objectives during the next 30 days. This plan looks at first blush like a well-organized system of attack, with all the strategy and tactics in place. This person then closes with, "If I can help any of you, please contact me." He—or she—leaves, and, within seconds, even the Shadow could not find this new Invisible (Wo)Man. The withdrawal type is never in the office, never returns phone calls. This person is not even around to blow out a birthday candle—let alone a real fire. You might say this manager is "missing in action."

The *acceptance* leader is equally useful in his or her own way, for this leader never said "No" to anyone in his or her life. If he or she offers to hire a new agent at $200 a week and the interviewee counters that $250 is the acceptable minimum: "You got it!" If the home office sends down word that this person has to hire two agents in 30 days: "You got it!" The acceptance leader will produce the pair on time, even if they do not know whether the ball is pumped or stuffed. This person wants to be well liked by everybody all the time—and suffers from the most virulent disease that can afflict any manager.

Finally, there is the *commitment* manager. This person attracts, instructs, weighs, evaluates, and develops. He or she itches with the desire to excel and parlays this urge into a thrust to develop excellent agents who will do what is supposed to be done, serve society well, and make a comfortable living in the process. This manager provides a solid role model while demanding exemplary conduct on the part of trainees.

Of course, we all would like to think we are commitment types. But I am certain that most of us have been all four types of managers at various stages in our careers. Always check for any slippage into *control, withdrawal*, or *acceptance*—for any of these three will diminish your leadership capabilities.

You must be a *commitment* manager to excel and be able to upgrade your agent's education. You need to gather all the patience you can muster and spend the time necesssary to bring out the best in your people. You must demand effectiveness more from yourself than from those who follow you and motivate all whom you teach to improve and to set high goals. Get all to think *big* and the results will be overwhelming. Always remember that you are on a mission, and to accomplish this mission you need goals: Start—carry through—complete.

11

The Debit Agent Versus the Ordinary Agent

For 30 years after World War II, the majority of us who can recall the era were enjoying one long party. Although there were exceptions, for the most part the economy was rolling along nicely, employment was relatively high, and the inevitable changes were neither dramatic nor traumatic.

The party is over. Changes that have already occurred promise both drama and trauma for the foreseeable future.

Consider the medical profession. Many physicians who had been making six-figure incomes have found their market shrinking, and not simply because there are twice as many doctors today as there were ten years ago. Wellness programs have been springing up all over the land. Competition is much keener. Doctors are reverting back to what until recently has been a forgotten possibility: they are making house calls.

And hospitals are now conducting competitive, multimedia advertising campaigns—but for a diminishing clientele. Medical centers have mushroomed to compete in an arena once the exclusive domain of hospitals. I believe that within ten years half the hospitals operating today will have lost the competitive race. They will have failed to provide the services demanded of them by their prospective patients.

The same applies to supermarkets. A generation ago they sounded the death-knell for corner grocery stores. But along have come the fast-food entrepreneurs—and the phenomenon of people eating two-thirds of their meals out of the home. To an increasingly astonishing degree, Americans are passing up home cooking, dish-washing, table setting, and clearing—chores—and, in the process, are bypassing the supermarkets. (It would be ironic if the eating-out trend were the forerunner to a revival of "Ma and Pa" corner groceries and the demise of the supermarkets.)

I could cite many other examples to illustrate the following observations about the debit agent versus the ordinary life insurance agent. The debit agent is now taking bows formerly reserved for the ordinary agent. What the debit agent has been doing the past 15 years or so has come into vogue.

Thirty years ago ordinary agents as we knew them from such companies as Northwestern Mutual, New England Mutual, Mass Mutual, and Columbus Mutual had a tendency to talk down to debit agents from Prudential, Metropolitan, National Life and Accident, Western and Southern, and Liberty National.

Debit companies were serving what was referred to in those days as blue-collar workers. The supposedly higher-educated agents in the ordinary companies dealt with the tonier white-collar class.

But the next 15 years saw debit agents expanding their knowledge and education while continuing to serve their traditional blue-collar clients on a regular basis. Meanwhile, ordinary agents were painting themselves into an ever smaller corner. Their client-agent relationship score kept coming up zero. They tried to compensate by trying to prospect higher and higher, only to discover their agent colleagues were all converging on the same five percent of society. These targets, meantime, were chronically exhausting their savings in poor to terrible investments. By shifting with every whimsical breeze in the financial world, the ordinary agents took on the appearance of battered hulks.

They also saw a jarring apparition: The once-disdained debit agents, while tending two days a week to their stock-in-trade blue-collar clients, began spending their other three work days elbowing into what had been the ostensible off-limits territory of the ordinary agents.

So, in the past ten years, there has been an erosion of ordinary agents in numbers far greater than in the debit field—now known as "home service." As I peer into the future, I see a decidedly rosier income potential for debit consultants. Their field has an abundant population, with fewer loans, a fair degree of economic stability—and their clients have been convinced of the importance of forced savings.

Generally, the immediate outlook for ordinary agents is anything but rosy. Just as feathers on a fast-moving stream, they have been swept along into a blurry territory of investments, bewildered and unsure. Long range the ordinary agent will do well, but he or she must get over a few hurdles first and then focus his or her future thinking on doing total financial planning for the client.

12

Investing in
Tax Shelters

As this is being written, congressional representatives, presidential spokespersons, armies of potent lobbyists, and sundry others are climbing over, around, and through the President's proposed tax reform, looking to protect their respective herds of sacred cows. I do not know how long this process will take. I do not know what will finally emerge—or who will or will not benefit financially.

But I do know this: 1) I do not intend to lose any sleep over tax reform; 2) sure as death, I will have to pay a hefty chunk in taxes; 3) I am glad to pay for the privilege of living in what I perceive to be the greatest country in the world; and 4) I believe there will be ample room left for sound investments to enhance the income of those who take the time and effort to think about what they are doing and *how* they should be investing.

On that fourth point, I would like to observe that the silliest thing a person seeking tax relief can do is search out and invest in a tax shelter—and forget about it. If the investment itself is not solid, it is not worth a cent. No one needs to lose money.

TAX SHELTER ATTRIBUTES

In investing, the prime consideration for a tax shelter is one that provides:

a) investment tax credit and tax shelter;
b) ultimate appreciation;
c) checks—that is, distribution to the investor of money soon after the investment is made.

These three interconnecting rules are based on my many years of experience in the investing arena. I own or have owned as many as 35 investments. The best of these have been in businesses. They have paid great returns, have produced appreciation resulting in generous capital gains—but gave me little or nothing in the way of tax shelter. In this example, the good provider has been the fast-food business.

Ironically, the worst investments I have made were in a different type of food enterprise, the sit-down restaurant. Three of these turkeys nibbled me, collectively, for $500,000 before I parachuted. From them I received an investment tax credit, depreciation—and a big, fat loss I had neither sought nor needed!

My fast-food and sit-down restaurants constitute the two ends of the spectrum. Now come my investments in oil, gas, and coal. These are high risk—in fact, more than 75 percent of all such investments leave the investor holding a bag full of zeroes. Admittedly, the empty-bag holder does receive a large write-off, often a two-to-one. If he or she were in a 50 percent tax bracket and invested $50,000, the write-off could be 100 percent. If the investor remained in the same tax bracket the following year, it would mean breaking even.

To me, this would seem like panning a couple of years for gold, not finding so much as one nugget, and then feeling lucky I got out with the same packhorse, none the better for all the wear and tear. But to break even is to go nowhere. You need to set your sights on *going up*.

The best tax-sheltered investment I made was in cable television, which gave me a two-to-one tax write-off in what proved to be a going business with tidy distributions. Capital gains followed my investment sale. It clicked on all three essential burners.

From a pure investment standpoint (other than one put into a business), I consider *commercial* (not private) real estate to be the least risky. It also offers an attractive shelter (via investment tax credit and depreciation). In the past 20 years I have owned a piece of roughly 30 individual commercial real estate buildings. All told, they have given me beneficial depreciation, appreciation, and excellent distribution, and have averaged a net return of 14 percent. And I have never lost any money in land and buildings.

Before you invest, make sure the investment—irrespective of any tax benefits—is sound. Follow this rule and you cannot help but minimize your downside risk.

I caution you about limited partnerships. I have been involved in a slew of them and I firmly believe that if you are going into a high-risk area, you should *not* involve yourself as a general partner. Although such involvement may result in added tax benefits, if "it" fails, you will go down with it. The *Titanic* was the luxury cruise ship of its era . . . for one trip. At least as a limited partner you are limited to the extent of your investment.

ADDITIONAL ADVICE

I would like to caution you further: Never invest more than you can afford to lose. The twin to this edict is: Never borrow to invest if you do not have equity to back up the loan. Also, be ever mindful of what I personally think is one of the major problems in tax sheltering.

In many limited partnerships promoted nationwide, the promoter raises millions of dollars in a real estate investment trust. Be sure to scan the prospectus, for, in the fine print, you may learn the promoter is putting ten percent of the $10,000,000 raised into his or her own pocket—right up front. That's right, $1,000,000—just for raising the money! He or she may be the general partner and may be taking on a lot of debt. But that person is also weaving a fat, cushy safety net before anyone knows whether the investment will even get off the ground.

I have difficulty with these kinds of investments, regardless of what tax shelters may ensue. Unless you know everything there is to know about the people, the project, and the promoter, cancel the appointment.

If a long-distance call comes in from, say, California, and a long-gone old buddy (in his or her opinion) excitedly tells you about the opportunity of a lifetime (wanting you to put up your money on a "surefire, ten-to-one returner"), tell the operator your caller has the wrong number.*

DOWNSIDE ECONOMICS

So much for the dubious opportunist. Now it is time to discuss downside economics for prudent investing. If you examine all the possible options available day-to-day in this country you will find that nothing minimizes your downside risk as does real estate. Now, you may say ground and/or buildings. I combine the two. Ground, in and of itself, is useless. You could buy ground in the Sahara Desert and in ten years it would show no appreciation. If you bought farmland five years ago for $1,000,000, you might find its worth today is $300,000. Long range, I think most of that land will come back to its original value. My point is—be very cautious about investing in ground alone.

I like real estate buildings with sound leases, from companies with good track records. Even if a company renting from you were to go out of business, there would remain the very good chance you could lease the building to a new tenant. This is why I like real estate versus investment in a stock or bond. Stocks have the highest degree

---

*Better yet, tell *the caller* you appreciate the coincidence of the call because you are down on your luck and you could sure use a loan. Take the receiver from your ear to avoid injury when he slams the receiver down without so much as a quick goodbye.

of risk once you leave what I call the "big tax shelters." I personally love the bond portfolio because I have found that tax-free municipal bond investments have proved 100 percent safe for me. They performed exactly as promised: They pay six, seven, or eight percent, tax free; then, upon completion of the term, they return the principal.

I am also very fond of zero coupon tax-frees; that is, a bond requiring an investment, say, of $300,000 that does not pay any dividends during a 12-year period. But at the end of the prescribed 12 years, the pay-off is substantial and attractive, compounded by the freedom from a tax bite. It is a minimal risk venture if the municipality offering the bond is reasonably alive and well. Even in communities lacking balanced budgets, I am aware of only two that failed to return on the bonds they executed. I will leave it to you to investigate these opportunities on your own and in considerably more detail. My intent here is simply to steer you in what I consider to be attractive directions. Even though there is no investment tax credit or depreciation on the vehicles I have been describing, there is a nice tax-free return, which, for those in a high tax bracket, is like double pay every time you receive a dividend—or a return if you are in a partnership.

INTEGRITY AND PERFORMANCE

Of pivotal importance is doing business with someone you know has integrity and a record of positive performance. Of the two ingredients, I would choose integrity over the prospect for return; it is that essential. Caution also is in order for investments that historically have paid highs of 12 to 15 percent return but may now be at the peak of their usefulness ready for a slide. Iron-ore mining in Michigan may never return what it has provided in the past 50 years. Investments in gold or silver certainly are not what they were several years ago.

Again, put a relatively little bit in a lot of places. Do not put all your eggs in one basket unless you are in charge of watching the basket.

Finally, I think it is both healthy and in order to have a good feeling about investing. Precaution can and should remove causes for running scared. Now you can enjoy the fruits of your investments as they flower. The truly greatest feeling, I believe, must go to the person who, at the end of his or her working years, can realize a ten percent return—well ahead of most of the investors in our society.

13

Every Business
Is the Same

I have been deeply involved in such businesses as manufacturing, steel, discount drugs, fast foods, sit-down restaurants, and various retail and wholesale enterprises; and I have been on the outside looking in at a major grain business. Based on this experience I conclude that every business is the same.

We all know that the bottom line—profit—is extremely important to all businesses. We also are keenly aware of competition in our respective areas and the market share in our geographic location. So, if it seems necessary to diversify the business, diversification will be implemented before losses are suffered.

KNOWING PEOPLE

As with the insurance industry, 95 percent of it consists of knowledge of people, with the same reality applying to every other business. Five percent stems from knowing product; 95 percent stems from knowing people.

Computers can work diligently and efficiently, but if the human

121

relationships are not working in *any* business, the results will be pathetic; everything will be jammed up in the people line, no matter how well the computers may be humming. What is needed is constant direction by leadership, to keep the human (vital) side of the business in continuous perspective.

To give credit where due, I commend personnel departments generally. They do a fairly good job of hiring, after poring over resumes, interviewing, and checking out references. Personnel people know a lot about marketing, about their product; and their knowledge is, by and large, reflected positively in the applicants they hire.

But beyond the hiring process the business threads of similarity start to unravel—especially in terms of training programs, which I have emphasized are inadequate.

I include companies with good credentials and fine reputations. So long as they are profitable and so long as their marketing and advertising is effective, they tend not to concern themselves with the demands of training their sales force. But mounting competition over the past couple years is drawing attention to sales training and the sudden discovery of its fundamental role in business death or survival. Some previously obstinate executive "mules" have been smacked between the eyes by the two-by-four of competitors either threatening to catch up or taking the lead (and the profits) through their better-trained salespeople. Regardless of the underlying cause(s) I am glad to see the resurgence in respect for a success factor that has, for much too long, been the object of painful neglect. But, again, of course, the catch to catching up on this score lies in not simply training salespersons but in training their trainers.

TRAINING IS VALUABLE

The moral is this: If your training is deficient, get yourself trained by a knowledgeable instructor, even if you have to switch jobs to find one. Tell your young acquaintances interested in a sales career—in our industry or in any other—to soak up as much good sales-oriented formal education as they can. Lacking this key ingredient, we are like a team without an experienced coach—just waiting to be beaten. Moreover, as the pendulum swings toward greater sales training expertise in the next five to ten years, as I believe will be the case, those who did not gain the solid background that will be required will find themselves relegated to the status of dodo birds—extinct.

14

Conducting Meetings

Among the 41 agents in my office there are five on our management team. The following is my philosophy for maintaining a successful operation.

When I was running the organization, we would meet for no more than a half hour every Monday morning at 8 a.m., usually at the office but occasionally for a 7 a.m. breakfast.

I prefer early Mondays because it follows the relaxation that goes with a weekend and it is the appropriate day and time to recharge the juices.

I limit the gathering to 30 minutes because, simply, that is enough time to cover whatever needs discussing. Furthermore, I do not want to tie up valuable, productive people in glorified gab sessions. They cannot be out making money for themselves, the office, or the company if their movements are curtailed unnecessarily.

The subject areas are also restricted, generally to three items. This is a manageable, absorbable diet. Go beyond this and it becomes self-defeating, too much to digest at one sitting. Also, no single subject may consume more than ten minutes.

I prepare the agenda. I sift through the possible priorities and glean them down to the most critical few. I never announce in advance what will be up for discussion. This eliminates carefully prepared responses and capitalizes on getting the spontaneous reactions I am seeking.

If the agency were to grow to, say, 50 in the management group, I would still meet with a relatively small number—the top managers—to set goals for the week and handle other pressing matters. This is a practicality, not an exercise in keeping distance from the others. If it is only for a minute or two, I studiously touch bases with everyone on the staff, every day. It may be no more than, "Hi, how's it goin'?" while passing a desk, to a more extended visit dictated by a given circumstance. It gives the whole group chance to respond in brief or at length. But they all have a crack at me, any and every day of the week—and they know it. This makes them feel good and keeps me abreast of the most important people in my business.

NO MEMOS

Among other nice things, this procedure precludes the writing of memos, a practice I thoroughly disdain and one I do not use. Memos kill too much priceless time, are frequently the subject of misinterpretation, and do not provide what I want—immediate feedback on whatever concerns me. If I am right there in front of a staff member, I am making a personal "high touch." I am maintaining eye contact and, based on the response, I can elaborate to clear away any misunderstanding.

I know of some (too many) businesses in which the employees never see the boss except at the annual dinner. In such an environment, all sides lose—employees, boss, business, and stockholders. You have to communicate with everybody on the team, continuously. How else can a manager know what is really going on? How can a manager expect high productivity when he or she does not know who is on the staff?

I apply the above policies toward my two secretaries. We, of course, confer daily. I set their agendas, zeroing in on the two or three most important items. As the day progresses and specified tasks are accomplished, new priorities are established. We never get everything done. There are always spillovers, which receive their priority ranking on the ensuing day or days.

On a more structured basis, I meet with my secretaries four times a year to review generally what we have been doing and where we are headed. I believe in accenting their positive contributions right at the start. The concerns, if any, come later, when I broach them considerately and calmly. As valued members of the team, I treat them with the respect their dedicated productivity deserves. And I never raise my voice to them.

Because their compensation is based on *my* performance (which their efficiency helps make possible), I have paid them well and have added an increasing bonus from year to year. Even if my productivity were to drop, I still would be inclined to increase their compensation. Often I have heard the observation that "All your secretaries do every day is work!" True, they hit the grindstone, bypassing the water cooler and other common, unproductive office socializing. I pay and give them bonuses accordingly—and listen to what they have to suggest in terms of doing our total job more effectively.

15

Keeping the "U" Out of Slumps

Winning is never final and losing is never fatal. Everyone who has ever lived has experienced what we all have experienced—a series of ups and downs. So when you feel like a winner, enjoy; and when you feel like a loser, understand.

Sometimes feeling like a loser is not only unavoidable but unalterable as well. This feeling is catching, like a cold that cannot be avoided. "It's goin' around so it's my time to catch one."

Colds *are* unavoidable, but feeling like a loser is not. Although not completely unavoidable, feeling "low" can be greatly minimized and kept to a minimum. Eliminating depression about business begins with an understanding of what really causes it.

An example of what may well bring on the feeling of complete failure in our profession is the agent who interviews three prospects in succession and is refused one-two-three, all in one day. The agent's brain chemistry starts bubbling on the wrong burner, helping that agent continue to feel like a failure.

MENTAL REHEARSAL

How can an agent positively affect the outcome of interviews, thus minimizing the feeling of failure? One way is by being prepared for the presentation. Personally, I suspect very few agents do enough in the way of mental rehearsal before setting off to approach a prospect. By this I mean you need to go over and over what you plan to say. If you increase the quality of your preparation, you will find a more receptive audience. *Think* of how you can ease into the conversation, make your prospect comfortable, slowly building a warm relationship.

More than 1,000 books have been published over the years on the subject of how to close a sale. And when I lecture, invariably I will be encircled like Custer at the Little Big Horn by agents who firmly believe the chiseled-in-granite doctrine that the close is the most important part of the interview. They virtually pant for "the secret." I say they have been sold a bill of goods. I will go a big step further—in your behalf—and counsel you to *avoid* any book, article, lecturer, or what-have-you who advises how to close a sale. They will addle your brain.

OPENINGS, NOT CLOSES

I ask: How are your *openings*? As I have said before, sales are made or lost in the first ten minutes of an interview. Normally, if the opening is pleasant, so will be the result (the close). You will not be peppered with rejections. Your end of the day will find you where you ought to be, feeling good about yourself. Slumps come from within, not from without. If you feel sorry for yourself and decide no one likes the way you sell, you are 100 percent *right*. They did not like you on *that* day. You *did not* sell well. It was no good for them or for you. This may be tough for you to admit, but admit it anyway. I have studied this condition for a long, long time. The agent who is steady—not great, but steady—is an agent who seldom feels like a loser.

If you were to conduct a survey to determine why the greatest productivity in sales comes from well-established agents, I predict you would discover the answer summed up in one word: years. Well-established agents have paid a price for the experience. They have honed their skills, prepared carefully, and cut down on the number of times they have felt worthless. They essentially have jumped—or bumped—over the slumps.

Of course, you can go to the opposite extreme by feeling like a winner for too long a time. Just as I hope you do not spend very much time feeling depressed, I also hope you do not celebrate victory for an extended period. It is natural for a young agent to celebrate after landing a sale, whether large or small. But keep the celebrating short. Plenty of statistical evidence supports the notion that winning and losing come in streaks. Consider this: If you have a couple of days of poor performance back-to-back, maybe it is nature's way of telling you to back off a bit. Take off a day or so to rethink your strategies and motivation.

BORN POSITIVE

I believe that we were all born with plenty of positive genes. Look at babies, for example. They all are fighters, always groping, reaching, striving to achieve. Imagine their titanic effort to figure out how to, and then to actually, turn over. And what a marvel to see them attack the spindles of a playpen as they raise themselves, hand over hand, until they are standing in triumph. Next, they are trying to walk, assisted at first, then waddling by themselves. Next, they are running. What grit! What unimaginable courage! People are born *positive*, not negative.

What you are doing now compared with what you accomplished when you were two feet high is literally less than kid's stuff. Sure, you were helped along the way by parents and relatives. You have such supporters now, in your family, friends, and colleagues. They will help if you give them a chance and if you do not waste energy disliking yourself.

While you look to a small child for inspiration, think about the achievers seated around the Million Dollar Round Table. In addition to possessing a high quality of life, they enjoy noteworthy tranquility. Could it be coincidence that their lifestyle and composure are rooted in sales to a large number of people? If an agent is caught in a 25-

to-50-case production a year, no way can he or she have the peace of mind of the colleague who is selling 200 to 300 lives.

Please carve this in hickory: You can harness your mind. Once harnessed, your activity will improve. Once your activity improves, your downtime becomes short time.

BE SELECTIVE

Do not become hypnotized by a great speaker, regardless of how good he or she may be. I have seen agents scribble page after page of notes during a torrid lecture, then almost fly by their own arms back home, committed to applying everything they heard to their methodology. Scrap the whole works and start from scratch. Pick and choose. When something "feels good," add it to your arsenal, ease it in. Add, eliminate carefully, gradually. As much as you try to absorb new ideas, give as much thought to analyzing what cannot or will not work for you. Remember, also, that a salesperson fails often over the years—but you are not a failure until you give up and quit the profession.

It also is important to keep in mind that most things are neither good nor bad, unlike the difference between peace and war. You have to decide what is good or bad for *you*. You are the result of a combination of experiences—of instruction from teachers, books, and other media—all aimed at your development as a human being. Ideally, you will acquire a high degree of maturity, a hallmark of which is being comfortable in a crowd as well as when you are alone. Think of how often we all have heard about stars who were aglow when they were center stage but who sank into the depths of despair when not performing. They could not handle their highs. When their teeter-totter was up, great. But when it went down—they crashed. You *must* keep your teeter-totter balanced.

16

My Mentors

The word "mentor" is being tossed around more today than ever before. Originally "Mentor" was a friend of Odysseus entrusted with the education of Odysseus' son Telemachus. Thus *Webster's Ninth New Collegiate Dictionary* defines a mentor as "a trusted counselor or guide."

To me a mentor is all that and more—a person who is an example for one to follow, who possesses such admirable traits as a high degree of integrity and the very important quality of caring.

Why does anyone need a mentor? I think it gives you an opportunity to focus on someone you respect and admire who cares enough about you to contribute to your success and growth as a human being.

You have heard the expression, "self-made." Supposedly, this type of individual climbed the heights all by himself or herself—alone, without benefit of assistance from anybody.

There may be such a person roaming the earth, but I have never met one. Whether or not we care to acknowledge it, we all are the product of many influences, none more so than the people with whom we come in contact. If we are fortunate enough to recognize and nurture positive influences, however jarring they may seem sometimes, we may count ourselves really blessed. Each of us needs good mentors, knowledgeable and experienced guides who give generously and freely of their time in our behalf. Looking back from the perspective of age 55, I am as awed as I am touched by the array of people who literally went out of their way to help me mature, who were determined in their desire to see me succeed. Incredibly, none of them owed me anything. Now, as a human being and as a business professional, I owe them just about everything. To them I gratefully dedicate this chapter. Its narration, I sincerely hope, will in turn be instructive and beneficial to you.

Jim Murtagh, a successful industrialist, is the son of a great man who grew up with my dad in New York and who was my father's partner in a corner grocery store in Toledo. Suffice it to say the Murtaghs and Savages had a marvelous relationship; I cannot remember one sad experience in all our years of acquaintance. Aside from the obvious values stemming from so cordial an atmosphere, Jim gave me critical lifts at a crucial period in my youth. At age 31—seven years my senior—Jim called me at the store where I was butchering part-time and invited me to lunch. Now, for a young man to be invited to lunch in those days was like getting a private audience with the Pope.

Jim picked me up but, instead of driving to a restaurant, he pulled over to a curb and got right to the purpose of the get-together. He told me he wanted to buy $75,000 worth of life insurance from me. It was the biggest "sale" I'd ever made, with a premium worth $1,200, close to half of the $2,700 I had earned during the entire previous year. Jim had and has many friends. He could have put his money with an established professional but he put it with me. He also signed me up—at age 31—and paid for a lengthy Dale Carnegie course. Then, gently, Jim told me that, probably because of my heavy involvement in sports, I had a tendency to dress like an athlete all the time, even when I was supposed to look like a businessman, an insurance agent. He glanced down toward my ankles. So did I.

There was the incriminating evidence: a pair of sweat socks. Score a hit for Jim. He did not have to belabor the point—namely, that dark socks were definitely more in order, as was a tie with sport jacket or business suit. Not fancy, not extravagant. Appropriate. When such a mentor is so anxious to see you succeed, how can the lesson not be learned? It stuck, as has my friendship with a remarkable man.

At the ripe old age of twenty-five I got the dressing down of my life from Monsignor Jerome Schmitt (to whom I referred to earlier in this book), a lovable but no-nonsense priest who blistered my selfishness. A great friend to this day, Monsignor Schmitt turned me around as no other.

Another profound influence was that of Monsignor John L. Harrington, principal of Toledo Central Catholic High School. "The Great John L." directed me in ways primarily more temporal than religious, although there was ample supply of the latter. As a young high school teacher, Monsignor Harrington taught me the value and necessity of being highly organized. As an instructor, I quickly learned the urgency of being on time for an assigned class, day in and day out. *Any* tardiness meant a direct trip to his office for a basic review of teacher responsibilities, *beginning* with punctuality.

In his youth, Monsignor Harrington—a strikingly handsome man with a classic profile—had a reputation as being just about the toughest street fighter ever to inhabit a decidedly tough East Side. He remained tough throughout his distinguished life. But he was eminently fair, a true leader and role model for the many thousands of youngsters put in his charge. He approached his responsibilities with impassioned seriousness and intolerance for any hint of disorganization or lack of enthusiasm. Toledo is a better place because of his tireless devotion.

Until his untimely death in his early 60s, Joe Grogan epitomized that delightful combination of Irish spirit, wit, and charm. He owned a Chrysler-Plymouth dealership and when I was 26 sold me my first really functional automobile, a five-year-old, green Plymouth with tires that did not deflate when I turned a corner. (Up to that point, I had been fixing tires once a week.) We had met by way of our mutual love of sports—I a high school coach, Joe an avid fan. Before too long we were huddled over lunch, I disclosing my desire to go into insurance sales. Joe encouraged me and, two n.onths later, took me to lunch again where, à la Jim Murtagh, he said he wanted to buy life insurance from me. Joe subsequently introduced me to a parade of friends and associates (referrals) who signed me on as their agent—not because of me, but because of Joe. His generosity toward Central High School, The University of Toledo, the city, and hordes of other causes had endeared him to legions.

Over the ensuing years I spent many of my happiest hours with

Joe, usually hurting from laughter at his unique humor. But although Joe Grogan probably had less formal education than most of my mentors, he was as astute as any in this treasured bunch. He had a sheer genius for simplification. He could analyze and summarize a complex problem in a witty phrase. His talent was so inescapably impressive that, in time, I gradually assimilated his methodology, looking for simplicity wherever a maze emerged. Joe's sudden death was a great personal loss to me for he was a friend, client, and great mentor.

Frank Cubbon, devoted father of a large brood and a spectacularly successful Toledo attorney (who went to night law school after completing his duties as an insurance adjuster) came into my life under peculiar circumstances. My dad's grocery store had been failing from the competition of a new supermarket. Corner "Ma and Pa" stores were giving way to the onslaught of the big, efficient jumbos. Like Canute trying to stop waves from rolling in, I was on the telephone weekends trying to sell meat and arrange deliveries. Sometimes, in this frantic, part-time activity, I would amass as much as $500 in meat orders. Through a mutual friend, Frank Cubbon learned of my efforts and called in a $115 order. When I delivered, Frank was not home but I did have the pleasure of meeting his wife, Babs.

Another delivery followed and I met Frank, one of the most confident fellows I ever had encountered. He was not arrogant; he simply exuded an almost tangible aura of self-possession and candor. I liked and appreciated Frank from the moment I laid eyes on him. He reciprocated.

The very next week, at his home, he asked what I did for a living, noting that I obviously did not deliver groceries full-time. I told him I was in the life insurance business, just helping my dad in the evenings. Out of the clear blue Frank said, "I need some more life insurance. Why don't you call on me?" The following week he placed an order for $25,000 worth of ordinary life with me. No one has ever responded that quickly to me in my business, before or since. The very next week he placed another order for meat—and $25,000 worth of life insurance. In the next five years Frank was the catalyst for more than $1,000,000 in insurance referrals. Great as all this obviously had to be, the best dividend I received was learning to emulate his confident manner.

Curiously, it was a layman rather than a cleric who proved the most influential in my religious orientation. Enter Dick Schoen, a paving contractor and owner, the quintessence of a successful person. The Schoens and Savages go back a long way together. Among other similarities, both are prolific. I grew up with eight sisters and brothers and have nine children of my own. But Dick is the proud and happy father of *15*! His rarity is also personally memorable in that he represents one of my very few totally unsolicited insurance clients.

Frank Cubbon, Dick, and I were on an infrequent golf outing together when Dick's phenomenal religious devotion provided me an example I could never forget. This was back in 1962, in South Carolina, where Catholic churches are relatively few and far between. Typically, Dick had scouted the area and determined that Mass would be celebrated at a nearby convent at 6 a.m. the coming Sunday.

With plenty of lead time, we were all up and on hand for the appointed hour and spiritual event. Moments ticked away without any appearance by the celebrant. Inexplicably, we were confronted with a no-show priest. Anxiously, Dick checked with the nuns and learned that a Mass was to be said in another hour at a community 40 miles away. Immediatey we were off, with Dick burning the tires down the road. I began to wonder whether we were headed for a funeral Mass—ours.

For those unfamiliar with the Catholic faith, especially as practiced in the early 1960s, it was incumbent upon the faithful to participate in the three principal parts of the Mass: Offertory, Consecration, and Communion. To miss one part was to miss the whole. We panted into the church only to discover, to Dick's complete dismay, that the priest was well into the Offertory.

Frank and I were completely secure in the belief we had done everything humanly possible to comply with our religious obligations. Not so for Dick—at least not until after he had gone to the priest celebrating the Mass, told him what had happened, and gained the priest's assurance that his and our obligation had been fulfilled. But it took a predawn rise, a frantic pursuit, and priestly counsultation to allay Dick's apprehension. Dick lived (and lives) his faith with a tenacious love that has no compromise. By example, he taught me more than I could ever learn by rote.

By the time I was in my early 30s I encountered a food industry legend, Virgil Gladieux. Virgil built a national food service empire from a Spartan beginning, which involved selling sandwiches to Toledo factory workers. Now well into his 70s, Virgil remains incredibly busy, both in his business and in a myriad of civic activities, especially for the city, university, and church. He taught me the art of fund-raising. He has a concise but self-revealing philosophy: give until it hurts. He does and gets legions of others to follow suit. In Virgil's canny view, giving until it hurts actually makes people feel good. Let people, he counseled me, be as good as they *want* to be in their giving, even if this entails stretching their payments out over five years. Virgil changed my giving habits and my way of looking at charities. Here is a man whose generosity is exceeded only by his wisdom.

So far I have revealed mentors who greatly influenced my ability to self-evaluate, to organize efficiently, to exude confidence, to dress for the occasion, to simplify the complex, to live a better life, and to work more effectively in behalf of charitable activities.

The following four men offered friendship and helped me immeasurably in the intricacies of running a business. Some of their names you will recall from my earlier references. John Anderson, with whom I have spent roughly 1,000 hours, one-on-one, over the past decade, is most likely the most open individual I have ever encountered. Eldest brother and titular head of the family-run The Andersons, John is well-rounded and very interesting. Our topics of discussion range from Plato to the janitor in a fast-food franchise. (I do keep one thing in mind when I talk with John, however: If I want a secret kept, I do not tell him what it is. His life is such an open book, he wouldn't know how to close it.)

Primarily because John is so above reproach, I suspect, he has had a wonderful life. His wife, Mary, is a joy, as are their ten children (another big-family man). If anything, the demands of parenting so large a family have polished his matchless instincts in caring for The Andersons' many employees. If ever there were a corporate father image, it is John. He is motivated by empathy and love, which is all he truly cares about in this short travel through life. But the temporal payoff for his business has been a happy, energetic, imaginative and productive work force.

John has been close to death two times and has the added perspective that comes from surviving extremely close calls. I am delighted to know he is physically stronger than he was a year ago and is looking forward to being father of the bride to three of his daughters within one year. (Try that one for an endurance test!)

John's brother, Dick (discussed previously), was a high school classmate with whom I was not very close at the time. He was two years older than I, twice as big, and ten times as mature. Dick holds the title for having the biggest handshake I have ever survived. Dick has the uncanny ability to "high touch" virtually everyone with whom he comes in contact, within or outside the thriving business of which he is the active head. He never asks more of others than he is willing to offer himself, which is staggering. No manager could be more devoted to his charge. For a man in his position, his income would seem laughably low in the view of many.

But, as with John, Dick is not moved by what money and perks can do for him. I have been privileged to be close to this man's man for many years. In hundreds of hours of discussions with him, he has given freely to me of his warehouse full of knowledge on what American business is and should be all about—everything from sales to marketing to management, up and down the line.

Fortunately for me, the same can be said with respect to two genuine stars in the corporate hierarchy, Stan Gustafson and Rene McPherson. Until his tragic death two years ago at the age of 52, Stan was CEO of Dana Corporation, a group that never sits still and that invariably seems to come up with a new and better manufacturing or service insight. Stan's mind was like a giant sponge. But his capacity to absorb limitless detail never put him beyond reach of *anybody* who worked under him. Moreover, he conveyed his intimate knowledge of everything that happened at Dana to all the troops with an enthusiasm, a sheer love of bustling activity that never waned.

The story of Rene McPherson sounds the same. Rene was Stan's predecessor at Dana and had a business brain that could only be measured in megawatts. A stunning, record-breaking achiever while at Dana, Rene retired at age 55 to fulfill a goal of being dean of the College of Business at Stanford University. Because of a nearly fatal accident, Rene left Stanford ahead of schedule, returning to Toledo and, thankfully, to active civic leadership and extended public speaking. It was through Rene's friendship that I was given an insider's look at Dana and at the people who make it tick. What an eye-opening opportunity!

My most memorable mentors in my own field include Price

Ripley of National Life of Vermont, who took the time when I was a young inductee into the Round Table to hone my selling abilities; Mike Gilley, who brought me into the life insurance business and who encouraged my father in believing I could make it; Ralph Waldo, president of Columbus Mutual Life; Ben Hadley, Ralph Waldo's predecessor; and Frank Neal and Frank Carter, also of the Columbus Mutual home office, all of whom helped me unstintingly along the way.

These good, thoughtful people have made all the difference in my life throughout the years. I am 55 and am still looking for the same high-quality instructors. None of us is too old to learn. After all, life is a journey, not a destination, and each of us needs help along the way. Keep your eyes peeled for mentors who can show you how to get in the fast lane on all the avenues that count: personal improvement, professional development, and peace of mind.

Having benefited so greatly from such wonderful advisers, I am eager and happy to pay my dues for this assistance, by helping, guiding, and encouraging others in need of advice or direction. I am truly grateful I have been able to assist many people in a variety of ways. Two examples of my efforts at passing the mentor baton include Ron Langenderfer and Phil Hoag. I had encouraged Ron to start his own steel company at a time when he was happily married, the father of two, and drawing a six-figure income. Yet I persuaded him to go into business for himself. Well, the jury is in: In eight years Ron has built a very successful steel company. In the process, Ron has developed as the most accomplished manager of any small company I have ever met.

Phil Hoag was one of my high school students. When he graduated from college he went to work for a national fast-food company. I had wanted him to come in with me, but it did not happen. Still, we kept in touch. One day he called and said he wanted to run his own business, as a franchisee of what I considered to be a less-than-promising fast-food operation. I told him as much the following day, after I had flown to New York to meet with him. Phil took my counseling to heart, shopped around, then found four Burger King restaurants available for purchase in Baltimore (at the time, I had suggested that this chain and McDonald's were the only solid options). I put together a partnership and financially backed him. Phil now personally runs 20 Burger Kings and is responsible for an additional 14. He is probably the greatest motivator and organizer in the Burger King company.

These experiences have taught me that, while it is great to be on the receiving end of helpful, experienced hands, it is really thrilling to be a successful mentor, knowing your input has made a significant, positive difference in those you want to assist. Try it. You will discover one of the most gratifying experiences of your life.

17

Questions and Answers

My purpose in writing this book is to touch on as many sound points as I could think of in attempting to show how you can improve your productivity, get more out of your profession, and live a fuller life.

I realized, though, that my writing was very likely incomplete—that I had failed to include, for one reason or another, questions that might warrant asking and answering.

So, to help cover as many points as practicable, I invited several insurance salespeople over to my house for an evening of potshotting—with me as the target. I explained to them that any subject in the repertoire was fair game and that they could fire away at will for as long as they wished.

Tom Snow (Maccabees Mutual), Dave Walker (Equitable Financial Services), and Mark Smigelski and Tim Croak (Columbus Mutual)—all young and successful—were gracious enough to accept my invitation and provide the fodder for this far-ranging chapter. I still may not have covered everything you might have wished to see. But, thanks to my colleagues, you will be reading more than would otherwise have appeared.

Question: How do you get to someone you'd like to have as a prospect? Say, someone you meet at a social event?

Savage: I never introduce myself as a salesperson on such an occasion. I separate my social life and my business life, my church life and my business life. Except for a new neighbor client who moved in, I have never approached anybody in the neighborhood for business. I have no problem with people who do. I just feel better not doing it. Now, I may well ask a mutual acquaintance to act in my behalf as a referral to a potential prospect. But I don't act on anything other than a referral.

Question: John, do you have a goal, weekly, for prospecting?

Savage: No, I have a goal for getting 100 new clients a year, with 70 secured before the start of summer.

Question: A new client is who?

Savage: Anyone who does business with me. I don't differentiate between policyholders and clients. I assume everyone's a client.

Question: Do you still do most of your sales activity in the first part of the year or has your system changed?

Savage: I used to do prospecting in February and March, very heavily. But now January, which is my biggest month, has moved over and totally enveloped February. So now March and April are my prospecting months. In November I do a lot of prospecting again.

Question: Can I ask you again, do you prospect for a whole month without actually having a closing and seeing clients, etc.?

Savage: No, no, I still see some clients, but not so many. I have never been able to do both very well at the same time. People ask "Upon delivery do you ask for names?" Never.

Question: You say you never call somebody unless he or she has been called. How do you keep track of that?

Savage: Well, I call a client requesting a prospect or two. The client may mention someone. I ask "Would you be comfortable calling him and talking about me and then I'll give him a call?" The call will be placed for me. I'll get the word and take it from there. I couldn't do business with someone who just came by without my knowing anything about him, without any references.

Question: When you first started prospecting this way, did you have any reluctance to ask people to do what you were just talking about?

Savage: As I pointed out previously, it took me nine years before I made $5,000, including renewals. So, I must have had a *whole* lot of problems in a lot of areas. I did a lot of things poorly. It doesn't require much skill to pass on what has been done poorly. Beyond this, I have difficulty doing what has traditionally been done. You know, they say, "You've got to learn the hard way." Or, "I came up the tough way, so you should come up the tough way." Well, we'd all still be swimming instead of building bridges. So, we should learn. I called The University of Toledo graduation class of 1954 and sold three people. I probably made 1,000 phone calls. You've got to be dumb to pass on that as a way of prospecting. George Aberele and I split it the next year. We each sold about five or six people.

Question: Do you keep records of people you called? What is your success ratio?

Savage: I'm just interested in results. I have a yellow pad I work with, all the time. I have a list of people to call. Now, on the prospect list, for example, is a fellow I've already had breakfast with and who I'll be seeing tomorrow. When I sell them or see them, I cross them off. When I left for work this morning I had 47 things to do today. They're all listed. I got 22 done. The other 25 I'll try to get done tomorrow.

I never get everything done that I say I'm going to get done in the course of a day. But I think I'm highly organized, although I'm not very neat. People often have trouble differentiating between the two. All I'm interested in is meeting the people and having them become clients.

Question: Suppose somebody says, "John, I just don't want to talk to you right now." Ever call that person back?

Savage: Never. If they say "no" to me, I never call them back. There are two kinds of sales: the easy one and the one you don't get. That's what I live with.

Question: What factor separates you from the other insurance people in Toledo? Why have you succeeded where so many others have remained more or less mediocre?

Savage: I think the comment is kind but I don't know where you get the information. I think my years in the business are the biggest factor. Over 34 years I built a clientele. That's our job. Building. I think if you're around as long . . . if you come to bat more often than anyone else, you'll probably become a better hitter. Now, I'm not disguising the skill or talent, which are God-given. But I believe I am unique in a special way: I think I work harder in our business than anyone else in Toledo.

Question: What's your definition of working hard?

Savage: I really believe I see more people than anyone else in a given year, in this community.

Question: So seeing people is . . .

Savage: That's the only job.

Agent/Statement: It's because you're so highly organized. It's so hard for me to have annual reviews because I'm not to the point where John is as far as organization. I'm doing a lot of the work somebody else could be doing.

Question: You raised a point here. John says he's organized in an unorganized fashion, but I heard what you're saying—that he's highly organized. Maybe we could talk about the mechanics of what allows John to get in front of so many people.

Savage: OK. How do I work, right? That's interesting because no one has ever asked me that. I have a breakfast appointment almost every morning. Seven o'clock. I meet someone for the first time. He or she has been referred to me.

Question: Can I get real basic?

Savage: Go ahead.

Question: What do you say to them? You sell yourself, basically?

Savage: The first meeting is just to get acquainted. My job of salesmanship is to get them in my office.

Question: It seems as though it's redundant to have two meetings instead of one. Why not get them right into the office?

Savage: I categorize you as a hunter rather than as a trapper. I'm a trapper. I have to get comfortable with someone first. But I want to talk about how I work, to follow the question. By 8:30, 8:45, I'm in the office. Nothing exacting about that.

In January I don't have any options because there's someone in to see me every hour of every day. My plan makes me work. I have ten appointments a day in January. Don't forget: They come to my office, I start early, and I end late.

Question: Out of those ten, how many do you set up?

Savage: None in January. They're all clients, set up by my secretary. I don't do anything that someone else can do. I have a luncheon appointment every day. I don't read mail. Probably 90 percent of my mail I never see; 85 percent of my phone calls I never get.

Question: You've trained your secretaries to do this?

Savage: Yes. Ever get thrown in the water when you were about seven years old? That's how they were trained. Interestingly, as soon as a client leaves, I dictate the essentials of the appointment into a dictaphone. My secretary then transcribes it, puts it in a file, and I don't see it until the next year. When the policies come in, I mail them, with a nice cover letter.

Question: Do you go over them?

Savage: No. But I do mail a personalized letter with the policies— not a canned letter.

Question: What do you do when you get a luncheon cancellation?

Savage: I go around and ask some of the agents if they'd like to go to lunch, on me, just to keep the flow of the activity. People who don't have good work habits are now being forced, because commissions are cut, to do twice as much to stay even. And I think therein lies the difficulty of the training. I don't think people are talking about 200, 300, 400 lives. And it's a must.

Question: If you weren't in the life insurance business, what other business would you want to be in?

Savage: I enjoyed teaching. I would be happy in a classroom. But, obviously, I wouldn't be eating as well, nor would my children. But I would enjoy anything that is people-related. I am very comfortable in the whole financial planning area, which is what I've been doing for 20 years.

Question: John, what motivates you to operate on the schedule you just explained to us?

Savage: I'm a goal-oriented person who can tell you this very honestly: I burn my plaques—and have for 15 years. I can't tell you the last time I read a company log to see who's close to me. Last December 1, I got a phone call that two people were going to beat me. My reaction was, that's good—who are they? I didn't sell for the rest of the month. I think it's equally good to be second, third, eight, tenth, or first.

Question: Recognition does not excite you?

Savage: Not at all anymore. Recognition was extremely important when I was new in the business, probably a burning desire when I was in my 20s. I think that's what made me competitive in sports. I enjoy competing. But I enjoy you beating me, too. Probably religious faith overtook competitiveness when I was in my 30s. A lot comes with maturity. I think you have a duty to work when you say you're going to work. So, I'm duty-bound.

Question: At what part of your prospect meeting do you say you get commissions only from the sale of life insurance, nothing else?

Savage: Very early. With a businessman prospect, under the right circumstances, it could even come at the breakfast session. I say, I do this, this, this, and this—no fees. The only income I get is from insurance sales and if you need insurance, I expect to be the agent. It's my source of income.

Question: Don't you think your high profile in the community helps you, John?

Savage: Yes, no question about it. How do you get the profile? I'd like to bet that if you asked 25 people in town about me, you'd get 25 different answers.

Here's an example. My kid gets a haircut Saturdays. One Saturday I was at the barber shop when this lady asked my kid, "Do you think you'd like to go into politics?" Like *I* was in politics. Aaron (my son) didn't even know what she was talking about. So, she'll probably pass it along that "Savage's kid is thinking about going into politics." Exaggeration plays a role.

Question: But at breakfast you can say, I've done this, this, and this, I'm in the business with this, this, and this. I can't say that. . . .

Savage: No, but I couldn't, either, when I was starting. It took time. But I'd still tell people the same thing. I wouldn't charge a fee if I were 21 or 25. I think charging a fee is short-circuiting yourself and will certainly limit your compensation. Creative, successful people get paid more than people who don't create.

Question: Many of the sales you make are sold on the basis of the saving element—is this a fair statement?

Savage: Yes.

Question: Do you spend more time selling people on saving or on the need side of life insurance?

Savage: There's no question I spend more time on the savings aspect. Not just life insurance, though. Total savings. Most people don't save money. In fact, I emphasize the bank over life insurance as the savings vehicle, without disregarding the need for protection. If there weren't protection we wouldn't be in the business. People, especially young people, think they're on a merry-go-round. A young couple will come in and tell me they have a house payment of $1,800 a month. Everybody tells them, "That's great!" I'm the only one who tells them, "That's awful!" When they ask me when they should buy a home, I tell them to wait two years. They wait two years. Somebody's got to straighten them out—or at least try to—instead of complimenting their spendthrift habit.

Question: John, many of us sell a lot of term insurance. But what does John Savage say to get people to change to whole or universal life? Or—to put it another way—how do you answer the objection that term insurance is the answer?

Savage: Term insurance can very well be the best answer. So, when someone throws a statement like that, I have to recognize that I sell a tremendous amount of term insurance. It affords great production over a period of time. But it's *designed* for short coverage. You wouldn't buy term insurance if you knew you were going to live to be 70. It's actuarially computed not to be in force when you die. And I use that line in every presentation. Secondly, if it were the best thing, that's what I would own. I own *no* term insurance. If a guy says he only needs it for a few years, then sell it to him. If someone comes in and says, "I believe in term insurance and investing the difference," you say, "Sign here." However, I have to ask myself about people who come in with fixed positions. And the question I ask is, why are they meeting with me? Whatever they *say*, in reality they *want* good advice. They didn't just pick my name out of the Yellow Pages. Our meeting should be a learning process. Some time during the interview they're going to ask, "John, what do you think?"

Question: Do you look for prospects in a given market?

Savage: Yes, but I also believe that every human being with an income is a market. Once I get in . . . well, I sold 12 clients in the steel business in a three-month period. I went from one to the next. It wasn't that I was searching out the steel business as a market; it just opened up as one. My biggest market, as far as income is concerned, is business people. But my largest *total* market is people who work for other people. Not business owners, not doctors and the like. The masses.

Question: I'm just finishing up three years in the business and I think the important thing is to stay motivated, to keep on making those phone calls. How do you run at a high level? How can anybody?

Savage: When you brush your teeth in the morning, be honest with the person in the mirror. I feel *good* about myself, about what I do for a living. So, if you feel good about it, you'll really be excited to get to work every day. Understand, you get to see a new face with every new prospect. Most people don't have that as a job. I think we're very privileged. In our business, failures get caught. For the most part, failures do not get caught at the big corporate level. Pretty tough in those places, with all the bureaucracy, to find out who's goofing up. But attitude, not aptitude, will always determine your altitude. I've said that many, many times. Your attitude about yourself, primarily. I have only two lives: business life and family life. I don't have time for more. My job is to raise nine good citizens, not be out with two other couples for dinner three nights a week.

Question: How do you sell so well—that is, with so few rejections?

Savage: Everyone talks about my organization and prospecting but no one talks about what happens at time of sale. How come virtually everybody says, "Yes"? How come last year only four appointments didn't result in a sale? It has to be what you're saying during the interview. Irrespective of what you may think, most people in Toledo have never heard of me. But people in the business think all I have to do is walk down the street and, like Ted Williams, the ball just hits the bat. But, what you say in the interview should be catching: "Boy, I never heard that before."

Question: Do you say the opposite of what they think you're going to say?

Savage: I try to be different. I don't think you have to gimmick it. I still say some day I'd like to sell encyclopedias by saying, "Folks, these are really good books and they cost $274," instead of throwing them on the table and saying, "Do you realize it costs you nothing, all you have to do is give me ten names . . ." You know—all the gimmicks, instead of selling the real worth of the product, which is a fine product. Marketing people would disagree, saying you have to tell everything but the obvious. That's where we part company.

Question: What about dismissals?

Savage: Sure, I get them, everyone does. But I also dismiss clients. Recently I dropped a client who had turned into an all-time pest. But do it tactfully. No point in upsetting anybody. My latest dismissal couldn't have gone better. He had an agent there when I went to see him who'd told my client I was doing a lot of things wrong (even though the client started off by saying, "John, I trust ya, I like ya, but . . .") and that he could do a lot of things right. I let the guy speak and then I told my client, "This guy's *good*. I think you're much smarter going with him. He's closer, etc." G-O-O-D-B-Y-E. It made my day.

Question: What's your perspective on total financial planning?

Savage: I think you have to do total financial planning to succeed in any facet of financial planning. If I were selling mutual funds for my income, I would do total financial planning, including life insurance, stocks, bonds. If I were selling stocks, the same: total financial planning for my clients.

Question: How do you stay on top of everything? Is it really necessary?

Savage: It's easy. There aren't that many facets of finance. There are many different products, but it's not your job to keep up with them. I hope you know this: There's just as much commission in a no-load fund as there is in one that has a load. The bank says, come to the bank, don't go to an insurance agency and pay a commission. But what are you paying at the bank? What you pay covers the light bill and rent and heat. I don't know why people have to apologize for making an income. We've let ourselves get caught up in the economic trap of advertising. People sit in front of the TV and honestly believe the guy who's saying, "No load." Wait a minute, I ask: You mean you make nothing if I do business with you? "Oh, I didn't say that." He'd have to say that because otherwise he'd be lying. What's wrong with that? The banks for years paid us five percent and invested our money at nine percent. Any idea of what kind of commission that is, from people walking through the doors? Tellers have to be paid. Bank presidents have to be paid. *We* have to be paid.

Question: You have a doctor you've been seeing for four or five years in a row, good income. Where do you go now?

Savage: Where do I go with this doctor who's bought a sizable amount of life insurance? (Let's say he has $500,000 to $1,000,000.) And he's *not* going to buy anymore. I *tell* people they've bought all they're going to buy.

I tell a lot of my clients that. I still see them every year. I think I owe it to them. Let's say his premium is $15,000 a year. I make $600 a year on that guy, don't I? Is it asking too much to have him come in for an hour? I get that for 15 years; in our agency we don't get anything after 15 years.

Question: You're not trying to sell him another product?

Savage: No, no. I'm never done selling. I may bring up the point that his wife now should have some more coverage. Or, he might start a program on the kids. But let's just say we have that all done. Then I would try to invade his pension plan for $100,000 of annuity because it pays 12 percent and there's not another vehicle in our society today that pays 12 percent. And I sell a lot of annuities inside pension and profit-sharing plans.

Question: How can you feel comfortable about advising somebody to buy rare coins? What have you done through the years to make yourself knowledgeable about other types of products outside insurance?

Savage: What I've done is found people who are very good in other areas and who are trusted, qualified people. I refer to these people.

Question: Basically, then, you just know the advantages of certain kinds of investments . . . rare coins, for example?

Savage: Yes, I like gold and silver. I have a lot of silver myself. I buy silver coins rather than silver bars—because the downside risk on silver coins . . . well, you can buy a Baby Ruth with a quarter, but you can't do that with a silver bar. If silver goes to zero and you go into a store with a bar, the guy'll hit you over the head with it.

Question: What about annuities?

Savage: I sell a lot of them. But, you know what you get paid on an annuity? Two-and-a-half percent commission. One time. I sold $100,000 for my company, Columbus Mutual, and I got $2,500. Now, you talk about a system of making money! Insurance companies pay 12 percent to the buyer, invest at 15 percent, pay you one and make two. But the customer still makes out the best. I make out the worst.

Question: How do you feel about IRAs?

Savage: A married couple buys a $3,000 IRA from you. What do you make? Seventy bucks. If they come in and stay very long, and are *sitting*, they're wearing out some of your furniture. You've got to be losing money—if the lights are on and the secretaries are typing—at $70 bucks an hour. But we do a lot of things we don't put a price tag on. You must serve *all* your clients' needs.

Question: How about when a client leaves the area, goes to Texas or California, say? Do you handle that or give it to someone else?

Savage: I give nothing to anyone else to take care of. That's the first answer. Do some other people get my clients when they move? Yes. Not by design. It's much more difficult to keep your clientele when they get away from home. I have probably 100 clients outside Toledo. But I started with 200. Still, it's better than getting into a pen-pal position.

Question: What do you do if your business is replaced?

Savage: Into the wastebasket. They've just dismissed me. When I've been dismissed, hey, that's part of life. They have the right to dismiss me. I have to be big enough to walk away.

Question: What if they just buy from somebody else? You've got two policies and somebody else sells them a policy. Do you stay in touch with them or do you just dismiss them?

Savage: Oh, no. I would hope the fourth time it's back to me. I'm after them with the best I've got.

Question: I've got a follow-up for that one: How do you maintain loyalty? I sense that it's harder and harder to maintain loyalty.

Savage: I think there's a transition, a restructuring of the whole area of finance. There are more financial planners today than there are buckeyes in Ohio. It's a popular thing to get into now. It has a lot more glow than being a life insurance agent. These people get some pretty good tapes, some decent training, and they sound good. So, competition is keener. I think building loyalty can only come by good follow-up procedure. That gets back to once-a-year reviewing.

Question: How often do you think an agent should take a vacation?

Savage: I do this better than anybody in the business, I think. I take a lot of time off. First, I'd rather not have to work at all. I could keep myself busy with a series of pleasures. I never work Friday night, Saturday, or Sunday, and I take my wife away no fewer than six times a year. Just the two of us. And, for the past ten years, I've taken off the three summer months. With me, vacations are extremely important to keep the balance. They are therapeutic.

Question: How about somebody new in the business?

Savage: You'd better not take any time off. If you're new in the business, you'd better go all out. That's what I did. But I always took a month off, in December, when business was down, anyway. I still think it's a great month for a vacation, especially for a young family. There's nothing better than the snow and the sleds and the time around Christmas.

I have to take time off to get going again. Subtract Sundays, I couldn't work for 313 straight days. I'd be burned up before I'd be exhausted.

Question: What's the best way for a businessman to buy life insurance?

Savage: The best way to sell life insurance is monthly, through the check-o-matic plan. But if the person doesn't like you to take it out of the checkbook every month, then it's the worst way to sell.

Question: I don't mean mode of premium.

Savage: I understand that. But using it as an analogy, if a guy says he doesn't like split dollar, then that's the worst possible thing you could go for. I happen to like split dollar, probably have more of it in force than anybody in this community because I believe so strongly in it. Now, what's better? I don't think anything's better, I think they're all good. I've sold many individual corporate guys on an employment agreement.

Question: Tell me what you mean.

Savage: I have an employment agreement set up for the corporate executive. In small corporations the owner is everything. If he's the president, his wife's the secretary-treasurer and she doesn't even know where the place is. I fund the agreement with life insurance. Never in the employment agreement does it mention life insurance. If it does, it qualifies as deferred compensation and you've got a PS-58 charge.

Question: What does the employment agreement say?

Savage: It says that if the executive is there one year, he takes $2,000 with him. If he is there ten years, the executive takes $80,000.

Question: What's the first thing a newcomer should learn about financial planning?

Savage: How to be financially responsible himself or herself. Those who were trained in my organization will tell you what I demanded first of them: Get $10,000 in the bank. I want to tell you, when you get $10,000 in the bank, you feel good. The first ten *really* feels good.

Question: That's not going to get that agent beyond the first month or so; I'm talking about the training part for the beginning financial planner.

Savage: No, you've got to understand that's part of the agent's goal, the long-range goal for a young person that has to be mentioned right away. In other words, how can "you" help "him" if you're late in your house payment? We've got to get rid of all those "if you's." You start by saying, "My personal financial house is in order." Now, when you're starting out in the business, nobody expects you to be in good shape financially. You've got to start when you're 21 to 24. At this age, you don't need much money. You may want it but you don't really *need* it. Then, you've got to see a lot of people, in an organized fashion. If a guy tells me he likes to send a lot of direct mail and loves to get on the phone and make cold calls, I'm not too sure of his future with me. That's my belief and it doesn't make it right. But think about how many people are made to do those things. Regardless, the young person coming into the business today has the same opportunities we had 30 years ago.

When I started, nobody liked insurance people. "What,

you're going into the insurance business? Can't you get a job? Wha'dya go to college for?" But I got into it, anyway. It was exciting and intriguing. Think about this: With insurance, if you die, your spouse gets a ton of money. If you don't die, you get your money back. Right there is enough to get me to buy.

Question: Does the high divorce rate complicate insurance sales?

Savage: It really helps the business. The second wife demands the same coverage as the first and the first wife is covered in the divorce settlement. Divorce has hurt our society, but it hasn't hurt our business.

Question: Do you think the insurance agent image has changed since you started?

Savage: The image has changed because nobody calls himself or herself an agent anymore. That's how important the image is; it's still terrible. "I'm a financial counselor."

Question: When I was in training, I was told to be proud to be an insurance agent. I've never been shy about saying so. I guess it's all in my head, right?

Savage: Oh, now you hit it all right there! All of our rejections are self-imposed.

Question: Part of my job is in management and the toughest part is in an interview where I have to decide whether this person is going to make it or not. How do you know when an applicant has the potential?

Savage: After years and years, you get better and better. Hey, if I could figure that one out I wouldn't be sitting here, I'd be writing a bible for the training session of the industry. I don't think you ever get to that position of knowing for sure who will or won't make it. You just try to evaluate fairly and objectively.

Question: How does a young person get past an older person's skepticism about his or her capability as a total financial planner?

Savage: An agent is more effective within a range of five years, up or down, of his or her clientele, for the most part. I do a lot of split work, mostly for younger agents bringing in older prospects. The split is 50-50. If I bring a prospect to a young agent, I may give that agent the whole thing. I do that with young agents. The difficulty comes at renewal, when they ask you to suit up again. I'm not looking for that kind of work. It means the prospect bought *me*, not the agent who brought him in. At this juncture, we both have to be very careful.

Question: To follow up a previous question, what are the facets of finance?

Savage: Stocks and bonds I categorize as one facet. Land and buildings, another—such as real estate partnerships, any land or building. Stocks and bonds, of course, incorporate the mutual funds, no-load funds, zero coupon bonds—all of what I call "the words of the day" that catch people. The third facet is any gambling—that is oil, coal, gas, tax shelters of any kind, gold, silver, coins, rare metals, precious metals. The other is all the retirement vehicles: pension/profit-sharing plan, Keogh, IRA.

Question: And to prioritize them . . .?

Savage: I think you have to show me you can save before you can invest. Savings, first. I think people are getting into IRAs who have no business getting into them. I'd bet 50 percent of the people shouldn't have an IRA. If you don't have $10,000 in the bank, you certainly shouldn't have an IRA. And young people really shouldn't have one, because they're in a 20 percent tax bracket, which means the government is putting in 20 percent, with the young person putting in 80 percent and locking it up until he/she is 59½ years of age. You can't get at it earlier without paying a penalty. Some financial institutions, I think, violate rules of ethics in their advertising. *Banks promote IRAs.* They promote a vehicle that—for the majority—should not be promoted. I mean, people putting $50 in an IRA. The guy who promotes that should be up for dismissal.

Question: Did you happen to read that article by (nationally syndicated columnist) William Safire, where he praised IRAs as one of the great savings ideas of the century?

Savage: No, but if that's his position, I'd like to debate it with him on TV, say, an hour on finance. He'd end up babbling. Sad, because I'm sure he's intellectually honest and thinks he's right. But those are the ones who are the most dangerous. They become zealots without really knowing what they're talking about. I'd be willing to bet that, ten years from now, there will be fewer than 20 percent of IRAs, bought now, still in force. Eighty percent will have been dropped or cashed in.

Question: John, to get back to what you were describing a while back about a young agent saving up until he or she has $10,000 in the bank—what monthly figure do you suggest?

Savage: We'd need to explore this kid's background (age 25, married, no children, both working, $43,000 combined annual income). I'd want them to save $400 a month. With that income, there's no way they couldn't save that amount. The question is, will they? Before we meet? No, unequivocally, no. After we meet, they will. It's a *comfortable* amount. And you're taking them from virtually no savings to a lot of savings. Eighty percent goes in the bank. In a year they'll have $4,000 saved, with interest. Twenty percent in insurance. The only kind for them is *permanent* insurance . . . young couple, no children. Then, if they do need term, they can extract that if they need the dollars to buy the additional coverage. Another example: He's 25, wife, $20,000 in the bank, $43,000 a year income. If I heard that in my office, I'd get up, give them a standing ovation, give them the chalk, and tell them to go to my board. That's how rare that is! But it does happen. When so, you tell them, "You're on your way! Now I want to introduce you to the world of investment. You are ready for some tax-free bonds." I'd put $5,000 in tax-free's and $5,000 in an annuity. So you get one as a tax-free build-up with a higher degree of return, with the other taxed when taken out. Two beautiful pieces of merchandise. Everything in the financial world is great. It's how it's placed. I'd also make sure they had adequate insurance (they may have plowed *everything* into the bank). I'd also ask: "Do you ever think you'll have a family?" They say they'll start in three years. At this point, I'd ask what they think of life insurance. Generally, the answer is to the effect they never thought much about it. To this I respond by advising that it would be smart to get some in motion right now.

Question: How do you get a person to commit to an annual review?

Savage: That's an assumed situation. I tell them up front that it's going to take us five or six years to establish a good economic base. I tell them I could just get them in here, sell them something, say goodbye, and never see them again. That's not good for either of us. We review every year, where they are, where they're going. "You're the one who's going to do it, but you have to bring it by me each year, that's all; a face-to-face relationship."

Question: How many people will come back every year?

Savage: Almost everyone. If they don't, no problem. They come back the following year. They won't come back if they've failed miserably in their goals.

Question: What's been your best case to date?

Savage: It involves a person who has been a good friend for a long time. Now, if you want to hear about something funny, it was me at 30 years of age, doing an estate planning job for someone who was 27 and had $30,000,000.

I boned up and went to him with this question: "Does it make any difference if you leave your kids $30,000,000 or $20,000,000?" Uh, uh. Didn't seem to make any difference to me, either. Then he asked if he really needed life insurance. I told him, no, but that I really needed the sale. And he bought $1,000,000 of ordinary life from me. And that was the sales presentation. I told him I made $19,000 from the sale. The rest of the story: He never bought any more.

Incidentally, Price Ripley at National Life of Vermont probably made the difference for me on that one. I told him I was about to make the biggest sale I ever made, $500,000 of ordinary life. Price was an astute guy, Million Dollar Round Table with a great reputation. He gave me some solid advice: "Son, there is no glow in a half of anything. Half an apple. Half a yard. Go there and sell a million. It's round. It's whole." I took Price's advice. I sold two $500,000 policies for the $1,000,000 total Price had recommended. They're still in force. The University of Toledo owns both policies. The University's the beneficiary and my client/friend pays the premiums. And it's a deductible item.

Question: So what's your average sale?

Savage: I don't really know. In total death benefit I'll do $50,000,000. Lots of little ones. Lots of big ones. I sell a lot of term and premium and convert term rather easily.

Question: How do you handle the client who wants to start withdrawing money out of the cash value?

Savage: We mail the forms and the client borrows out of the cash value. Because I have annual reviews, this doesn't happen very often. Last one was probably ten years ago.

Question: How do you determine which to sell, ordinary or universal life?

Savage: The amount of coverage has a lot to do with it. Age is a factor. Most of my premium dollars are purchasers older than 60 years of age. All ordinary life. I just got universal life myself at age 54. I find that 60 is roughly the cutoff for universal life.

Young persons coming to me, over the next few years, will probably all buy universal life. Next week I'll be talking with two people, one's 69, the other's 67, and we'll be discussing $2,000,000 on each person. And they'll be ordinary life, not universal life. Interestingly, each of these gentlemen has only a $500,000 coverage, despite an income last year, for one, of $4,000,000. Left as is, his death would be a tremendous blow to his company. Probably should have $10,000,000 coverage, but you have to use judgment when the price starts nearing the prohibitive stage.

Question: What are these "extra" services you provide to business people, beyond financial planning and insurance sales?

Savage: Marketing their product, conducting sales training sessions. See, most of my talks are outside our business.

Question: You're talking about your own clients? That is the first time I've ever heard this. This is fantastic! It's a dynamic sales tool that obviously eliminates competition. Tell me more about it.

Savage: Friday I spoke to a computer company in Minneapolis. I've given a number of sales talks for Dana.

Question: Wait a minute, wait a minute. Let's back up here a bit. Most of your business is with small, closely held businesses. Not the Danas, the IBMs. Now, to a prospect, you say, "I make my living selling life insurance, but I do all these other things." What other problems do you handle for them? Legal problems, trusts?

Savage: Oh, no. Other agents do that. *You have to be different from every other agent.* It started with The Andersons. Have you heard I do any business with The Andersons? This week the company has 15 hours of my time. I'm structuring two things there, one of which I can't talk about, but it's very big. The other involves working with their sales organization. Sales training and methods. Huge meeting in the fall—all their employees, all the spouses of employees of their retail stores. I've been involved with The Andersons for 14 years and they've never written me a check, for all the meetings and all the hours. But I do financial planning for a lot of their employees. So you come in with a good reputation. They're not mandated to do business with me. I've never written any insurance for the principals. But I have done business with many of their employees. McDonalds—I've written a lot of business for them, but never for the corporate top.

Marko Wholesale, ever heard of them? Well, I was referred to them, via Bert Rose to Carl Despero. I met with Carl, who said, "John, Bert is pleased with everything you've done for him. Tell me, what *do* you do?" I told him I do a lot of speaking. For instance, I find a lot of companies where the morale of the general employees is bad. Carl liked the sound of that. We arranged an appointment and I spoke at their Reynolds Road store after closing time, to all their employees and spouses. My topic wasn't insurance or financial planning. It was personal development—are you happy at your job? Are you excited about what you do? It went well and Carl was delighted. To make a long story short—two months later I told him I'd show him what I do in the area of personal finances. They've bought a lot of coverage.

Question: You never went after him to sell insurance in your first meeting?

Savage: No. That's when you take your time. But it wound up with Carl telling me I'd be writing whatever insurance Marko bought. And that's the way it's turned out. The next guy who goes in there trying to sell insurance is out of business. I went in there and used my talents in other areas. I've been doing this for about five years. I contend you have to do something for a prospect nobody else can do.

Got on a plane a month ago and bumped into a fellow I'd

been with in high school. Asked where he was going. China. Turned out he runs a Toledo-based company. He asked where I was going. I told him I was on my way to give a talk. What about? I speak on the major problems in industry today inside the corporations. (It just happened to be a new title I conjured up on the spot.) Well, you could hear his antennae sliding up to the limit. "Tell me," he almost yelled, "more about *that*." So I told him. Three months later—*never* be in a hurry—I called him. Had lunch with him today. He bought, after I told him that, while he was in high tech, I could bring in something his company didn't have, "high touch." I'd asked him what 90 percent of his company problems amounted to. Answer: communications . . . people. He'd spent an adult lifetime learning technical things, not in learning how to deal with people. Companies now are becoming very aware of the need to fill that gap.

Question: You have "little guy" clients?

Savage: Yes and I get a big kick out of this side of the business. Had a man in recently who described himself as just a poor worker. I told him never to say that. He had a wife and two kids. I said, "You've got it together." He glowed. His house payment is $94 a month. He's happy, he's excited, he's doing a good job.

He's got a physically tough job, tiring. But he's bright enough to want to know, intelligently, what to do with his money. Most people don't have any to put anywhere. There's a beautiful client. How much insurance? I probably made $200 from him. But the point is, there's more fun there. I'm reaching the masses through the vehicle of the classes. This leads me to tell you this—where the practitioner is missing the boat. It's worth your trip here tonight: The debit companies may very well rule the business in the future.

Look, here's Massachusetts Mutual, Connecticut Mutual, Northwestern, the Maccabees, the Equitable, and State Farm. Now, all their agents are moving toward the big sale, the professional upgrade. "Make sure you're talking to people with more income." But down below, where the little people live, there is no competition. What I've done is say goodbye to "up there" and moved to "down there." Where they all buy. And nobody's going for this clientele. This is 90 percent of America and it's almost untouched. I met an agent recently from Southwestern who's in the debit arena—and he's making $80,000 a year. He takes care of his debit Monday and Tuesday of every week. Door to door. Wednesday, Thursday, and Friday he gets a little bit and then he comes back to his nest. And nobody gets to his clientele. He's there every week, like a watchdog.

Agent/Statement: I agree. I was in Tiffin last week and made a sale. Every time I go to a little town, it's the same story. No one ever sees them. There's no competition.

Question: Why the referral method of prospecting and what is the procedure after meeting the prospect?

Savage: I think the referral method is the most professional way of doing business and it is a way of meeting people under the most favorable circumstances. Most people need help in financial planning and welcome your guidance in suggesting a plan that will ultimately determine their economic security.

After becoming clients, most people never see their financial planners. From a practitioner's point of view this is really sad because we know the largest policy one purchases is the last one bought. So if the agent does a tremendous job of service, he or she will be there to ultimately get the reward.

Stockbrokers engaged in total financial planning seldom see their clients face-to-face. Most stockbrokers contact prospects and clients by telephone and carry on conversations by phone over a number of months. Anyone who operates in this manner cannot compare with a person who faces a client on an annual or semiannual basis.

If you are a professional planner, never hurry through the first meeting and never try to sell a product the first time you get together with a prospect. People really appreciate your taking time with them—and you will find it comparatively easy to set up the next meeting at your office. I am very emphatic about urging that you set up appointments in your office and not at the client's home or office. I have been operating this way for the past 25 years and the results have been fantastic.

If you are comfortable with each other, the stage is set for you to ask, "When would it be convenient for you or for you and your spouse to come into my office, during the daytime or during the evening?" Most people will reply, "Any hour will be suitable." If that is the case, arrange a daytime meeting. For those who can meet you only later in the day, set up a 5:00 or 5:30 afternoon meeting. You should stay away from late evening meetings as long as you possibly can, unless the situation is exceptional.

Here are some guidelines that I highly recommend you consider adapting, for they have worked for me so successfully over the years.

1. If you are meeting a young single person, do not talk death benefits. Emphasize living benefits with a high concentration on savings.

2. If your prospects are newlyweds, make sure your emphasis is on setting up a short-range plan of savings. Make them aware that after five years you will be getting into long-range planning. They will appreciate your advice on getting some discipline into their financial plan.

3. For family people, talk about planning for now and in the future, and about living benefits and death benefits. If they are in their 30s, emphasize the importance of putting dollars away for their children's education. Those in their late 40s are concerned about retirement.

4. If they are near retirement, discuss with them the importance of staying liquid, conserving their monies, and avoiding risky investments.

5. If they are extremely wealthy, talk about the importance of estate planning to conserve and to distribute their estate assets for their heirs.

6. If they are business people, make sure you tread lightly on recommending major changes in business agreements—unless they are obviously concerned about that. I have found that I am successful in talking about the businessman's personal situation and then gradually working into his business. Do not ever be in a hurry to make the big sale. It will come if you do your job properly. I make it a point to meet with good business prospects between five and ten times during the first year. Often I will be

involved in five meetings, talking about their problems to see how I might be able to help them in their business, before I ever entertain doing anything that will compensate me. Winning over new business people is the most important thing on my mind when I engage in my first meeting. Many times they will do business with you over a ten-year period. You will be paid handsomely for taking the long range view. I repeat, do not be in a hurry to make that first sale. They will jump at the opportunity to deal with you, especially if you have been referred by another top business person. That will also hold true if you want to follow through with employees of the business owner. If you have been recommended by the boss, the employee will sit down and have a pleasant breakfast or lunch with you. Then, of course, go through your presentation as you have in the past.

Savage-isms

With a few exceptions here and there, I make no claims to having originated the following one-liners. Each is significant to me in some way and illuminates some area of my own personal philosophy and code of living. Please feel free to adopt or adapt as many as you want.

Work eight hours; sleep eight hours; just make darn sure it isn't the same eight.

Give a child a fish, feed him for a day; teach him how to fish, feed him for a lifetime.

Winning is never final; losing never fatal.

In the land of the blind the one-eyed man is king.

Worry is misplaced thought.

Number one, don't sweat the small stuff, and number two, it's all small stuff.

Business will continue to go where invited and remain where appreciated.

There is no competition in the world. If you can start something, carry it through, and complete it, you are in the two percent of our society.

167

Character and reputation seldom have anything in common. Character is what you are. Reputation is what people think of you. Never give up the former for the latter.

Intelligence is quick to apprehend as distinguished from ability, which is the capacity to act wisely on what has been apprehended.

I think the tongue was put in the mouth to keep information from others, rather than to speak.

The race of life is never won by the swift, rather the sure.

Athletics is a window that the public can look through and see a university—and a window that the university can look back through and see the public.

A friend is someone who knows you really well and likes you anyway.

Belonging to high society is like scratching something that doesn't itch.

The road to excellence is always under construction.

Never prepare a long written speech. Speak extemporaneously. The truth is always with you. You have to create lies.

We all have a compass within us; follow your gut feelings.

A negative thought is a down payment on an obligation to fail.

There is utility in futility.

After everything is said and done, more is said than done.

Character is easier kept than recovered.

An ax with a dull blade will do more to bruise than to polish.

People who don't make mistakes always work for people who do.

Man was not created equal. That appears in the Constitution—not in the Bible.

A clock watcher remains to be one of the hands.

Dogs by instinct turn aside when they see a ditch too deep and wide—not human beings.

It if ain't good for the swarm, it ain't good for the bee.

If you are tense, work. If you are anxious, work. If you are depressed, work. If you are happy, work. The greatest prayer is work.

It takes no skill to criticize. The skill is not to. I have been in 23 countries and have never seen a statue of a critic.

Most people live lives of quiet economic desperation.

I tell my children if they are in a small boat on Lake Erie and a storm comes up, pray to God but row to shore.

If you serve the masses, you will eat with the classes.

Every small business is the lengthened shadow of one person.

No man is useless while he still has a friend.

I do not know which is worse—not getting what we want or getting what we want.

In basketball it takes more skill to coach offense than defense, because in offense you have to handle the ball.

Man's business activities can be likened to the bird family—hen, ostrich, eagle. The ostrich never gets his head out of the sand and the hen flies low and heavy—only the eagle soars.

Solvency is a matter of temperament, not of worth.

Honest effort is always rewarded.

Of all the ships on the seas, the one most scarce is leadership.

Always be kinder than necessary.

We all drink from wells we didn't dig.

Be wrong so others may be right.

A good manager is not a person to lean on, but a person to make leaning unnecessary.

Shout praise and whisper criticism. (Good for any manager or little league coach.)

A hundred fools will never equal one wise person.

I believe that power does not corrupt people; corrupt people in power corrupt power.

For the thousands that are hacking at the branches of the tree of financial planning, there are few striking at the roots.

Abstinence is much easier than temperance.

People don't buy insurance. People buy people.

Whatever we have is a gift from God.

If you want to feel good psychologically, have more wins than losses. Every time you do something for another person, it is a win.

Golden lads and girls all must, as chimney sweeps, come to dust.

It is absolutely impossible to be thankful and be depressed at the same time.

If you go the extra mile there will be no traffic jams.

Know-how will always outdo guess-how.

You manage *things;* you lead *people.*

Be bigger than the incident.

Don't do what you like to do; like what you have to do.

It is not the company you're with, but the company you keep.

You only have one time to make a first impression.

Dress so no one notices; then, you are properly dressed.

Celebrate when you are up; understand when you are down.

Relinquish your ego.

Be a lead dog; it's the only way to get a change of scenery.

How is your listening-to-talk ratio?

Let people learn of your qualities and achievements from someone else.

You don't do by learning, you learn by doing.

You can't do anything about a person's actions, but you can control your own reactions.

If the channel is low on water, it is not the fault of the stream but of the source.

All you have to do to make it is last.

You must learn to handle bad news—you don't have to think it.

Get what you want by giving them what they want.

Afterword

I hope that after reading this book you will have a burning desire to improve and a full understanding of how important it is to build healthy relationships with all with whom you come in contact.

There is no "final chapter" in *High Touch Selling*; no diploma or degree or even signposts to mark your progress. "High Touch Selling" is a continuing process and the measure of how well you master it goes beyond material success.

If you are so inclined, try to spend a few moments every day in a prayer and do not be afraid of overusing the prayer of petition. I think you will find that with deep spiritual insights you automatically will promote tranquility within your chemistry. Equally important is your prayer of thanksgiving for all that you have to be thankful for. Express your love to your spouse and your children often. Try to do things for other people where there is no return possible. In other words, practice the art of giving.

I would like to close by adding a very important one-liner to incorporate—"Be quick to trust, be quick to love, and be quick to excuse."